GRANDMOTHERS
OF GREENBUSH

Josephine Guidera Licali and daughter, Ninfa, 1905

Recipes and Memories
of the Old Greenbush Neighborhood
1900–1925

Greenbush...
remembered

Catherine Tripalin Murray

Copyright 1996
Greenbush...remembered
1421 Wyldewood Drive
Madison, Wisconsin 53704

Library of Congress Catalog Card Number: 96-94510
ISBN 0-9626346-3-8

Design, layout and illustration
Alice Murray Luckenbaugh
Starlight Designs

Photograph reproduction
Tim Romano
Historic Photo Service

The recipes in this book have not been tested and
are featured as provided by contributors

Printed in the United States of America
by Palmer Publications, Inc.
PO Box 296
Amherst, WI 54406
October, 1996

Published by
Greenbush...remembered
1421 Wyldewood Drive
Madison, Wisconsin 53704

Other books by Catherine Tripalin Murray:

a taste of memories from the old "Bush" Volume I, 1988
a taste of memories from the old "Bush" Volume II, 1990
a taste of memories from Columbus Park, Volume III, 1992
Recipes of a Lifetime, Wisconsin State Journal, 1995

To my grandmother,

Catherine DiMaio Tripolino,

who went to heaven

before I was born...

ACKNOWLEDGMENTS

I believe that dreams to compile a book of this nature blossom for a reason. They are not designs drawn on paper on any given day, or ideas enhanced by other publications, but instead sprout innocently from the hearts and minds of artists whose quest has personal attachments. For me to capture a past beyond reach, a neighborhood that no longer exists, and a grandmother I never knew, the project became a nourishment of the soul.

The formative years of the Greenbush neighborhood that skirted Lake Monona and branched into a triangular shaped neighborhood, is the foundation for this book. Its major ingredients, other than fried eggplant, matzo balls, and sweet potato pie, are the women who became the strength of each dwelling on every court, street, and avenue. They are women who became mothers during the first quarter of this century by conceiving our parents, carrying them in their wombs, nourishing them with love, then welcoming us with love, years later, to complete their cycle of fulfillment.

It seemed so natural to feature the grandmothers of Greenbush as a way to capture the past. However, so much time had lapsed since the neighborhood had disappeared that making necessary connections was often impossible. Announcements made in Madison newspapers, club newsletters, and other ethnic publications drew little interest. So, as usual, I depended on the famous "grapevine" of conversation as a method to reach out. There are many who are not included in this book, but those featured represent them.

Friends from the Italian community who knew my grandmother tucked me under their wings and carried me back to the old days with poignant stories of the past. Anne Bruno, Lucy Corona, Mary DiSalvo, Bea Uccello Gervasi, Catherine LeTourneau, as well as the Gambino and Urso families, and the late Sarah Nietupski, often were my strength. Sam Onheiber became an enthusiastic representative of the Jewish community, while Francie Saposnik alerted readers of my endeavor in the Jewish Monthly Reporter, thus allowing me to reach beyond the spectrum of members of the Italian clubs and their monthly newsletter, Italia. Bernard "Bud" Sweet's book documenting Hirsh Selig Schvid and Esther Rachel Schvid and their offspring, opened a door for me, and Russell Pollock listened carefully, then allowed his book to remain in my possession for the long three year period needed to complete this book. Al Dockery shed light on the Black community, while others shared what they could.

Sincere appreciation extends to niece Alice Murray Luckenbaugh of Akron, Ohio for her artistic talent, design, layout, and beautiful grapevine illustration depicting a vital ingredient of many Greenbush backyards; Tim Romano for his personal interest and photographic reproduction; Leah Intravaia Younker of California for the sketch of her grandmother; and Jerry Minnich, for his professional guidance.

My husband, Dick, who has been so supportive of my seemingly endless efforts to make connections with the past, spent three long years trying not to interrupt my thoughts while I sat before the computer, and remained silent as I jotted down sentences in airplanes and hotels, on place mats in restaurants, or any tiny scrap of paper before sentences eluded me. And to my parents, Mike and Mary Tripalin, ever so proud of each accomplishment. My gratitude to them is with the deepest of love.

Stirred between the pages of the often misunderstood melting pot of Greenbush is a rich broth, simmering in culture, seasoned with kindness and love of those who cared, now being served to you with great pride. Once again, food becomes a common thread that binds us all. Some may have thought urban renewal would erase the past of humble ethnic settlements, but it is impossible with the old Greenbush neighborhood, for it remains the heart of fond memories and continues to beat with indescribable passion...

TABLE OF CONTENTS

cover photograph
Catherine DiMaio Tripolino

PASSAGE TO AMERICA

"I paid a visit to my 88-year old mother in the summer of 1962 and found her failing in body and limb, but mentally alert and responsive. It was with great delight that I maneuvered her to talk again about times past and the details of her years with my father. The problems of raising a large family seemed as fresh and vivid in the re-telling as I am sure they were in her mind and heart. The one incident which gives me the greatest joy somehow typifies my mother as she is today. 'Foreign-born' and holding on to her old country ways, my mother schemed and managed to arrange things so that my father took the credit for her sharp wit and her ability to 'play the angles.' Frankly, if this incident had not happened, I would probably not be here to tell about it today."

"My father, in the days of their early married life in the Province of Palermo in Sicily, was a hired hand for a wealthy farmer in vineyards some distance from where they made their home. There never was an overabundance of food, but the five children who had been born to them were healthy and active, and it was only the hard work and shrewd planning of my mother that made them so. About fifty years ago or more, as was the custom in the village, my mother would sit in the sun on the front stoop, crocheting and visiting neighbors. A peddler appeared down the street shouting, 'Little piglets for sale, little piglets for sale.' My mother spied what she calls a 'beautiful' little pig which took her fancy, and she entered into a bargaining session with the peddler. He wanted ten lira; my mother in her 'naive' way said she could only give him five lira. I can only imagine the bickering that must have gone on. Eventually the man left, saying she wanted to put him out of business. However, my mother remained calm and placid. She had a feeling he would return. Sure enough, the following day he knocked at her door and told her the piglet was hers for the five lira she had offered."

"Then my mother was really in a dilemma. Where was she going to get five lira? On the spur of the moment, she decided to borrow the money from my father's employers. Calling the eldest of her sons, she told him to immediately contact them and say that Mrs. Raimondo desperately needed five lira. Of course, this was all going on without my father's knowledge or consent, as he came home only on weekends. Well, the bargain was consummated. She had her pig. Next came the problem of breaking the news to my father. Of course, she had to face up to it and I can imagine the way she buttered him up before exploding the bomb. My father now had the burden of paying back the five lira plus the extra it would take to feed the pig."

"My mother took it all in stride. She calmed my father down (as I have seen her do many times) and told him that the pig was her responsibility and he was not to worry about it. She said it was too nice a pig and she had to have him. The way she tells it, the maneuvering must have kept her awake nights. She sold eggs from her flock to get money to buy food for the pig. The children were shortchanged a little, but they all looked forward to the future when the pig would be more than just a drag on the budget."

"My mother insists to this day that the pig was beautiful. He was getting fatter and fatter and she kept her eye and ear open for an opportunity to sell him. My father suggested she wait until he was a little bigger. My mother kept her peace at home. Finally the opportunity arrived and, as usual, my father was not at home. She had to bargain again as she did before. Only this time she had to get top price for her prize pig. The surprise came on the Saturday when my father returned from the country. Naturally, he asked where the pig was. My mother replied that she had sold him. My father, quick to anger, told her she should have waited until it was fatter. My mother said she had made a good deal. When she told him that she sold the pig for 100 lira, he sat down astonished. Here was enough money, after paying off the loan, to take him to the United States where he would have the opportunity to raise his family and give them all the advantages he had been denied and they would be denied if they remained."

"So that is how the Raimondo family got to the United States. My father, of course, came alone. When he had a job and a house he sent for the rest of the family. I came along a few years later and claim to be the only real surviving 'American' in the family."

"And that is why I say I am here as the result of a pig and the ingenuity of my mother. God Bless her."

Written in 1962 by Providence Raimondo Warne.

Submitted by Sue Greco LaBella,
granddaughter of Vincenza and Salvatore Raimondo

Ida Moskowsky and her dog, "Judy."

*Josephine Licali and her four daughters—
l-r Elizabeth, Victoria, Josephine,
Ninfa and Maria.*

Bella Sweet.

*Shivers family four generations. From l to r.,
Stanley, Else, David, and Mike.*

Bessie Sweet Onheiber with David. 1946.

*Conchera Salerno Raimond picnicking
at Hoyt Park.*

John, Mamie, and Steve Caravello, 1967.

X

l to r. Mrs. DiMartino, Mary Vitale and Mary Caruso. 1934.

*Catherine Tripolino with her first grandchild,
Elaine. 1934.*

*Chaika Sweet,
holding a
stringer of fish.*

*Josie Magnasco Schuepbach
preparing spaghetti and meatballs
in her restaurant kitchen.*

*Antoinette DiModica Stassi with
granddaughter, Joanne. 1951.*

*Property at 752 W. Washington
Avenue where Ben Setlick's family
resided on the second floor over
Charlie Cefalu's Shoe Repair business.
It is but a hint of the togetherness of
the Greenbush neighborhood.*

*Victoria Licali Salerno with grandson,
Nick Cuccia, in the backyard of the
Salerno home at 1006 Spring St.*

The "Bush" was not without fault,

but what neighborhood is?

Maybe we didn't realize how special it

was until it began to disappear.

INTRODUCTION

My grandmother died a week before I was born. I never had a chance to feel her hugs, hear her Sicilian songs, see her smile or discover the twinkle of pride in her eyes that would accompany the love she was waiting to shower me with. I missed not having her rock me to sleep at night before being tucked between hand-embroidered linens carried in a wicker container from the the land she loved. I missed not learning her dialect and spending time with her when she prepared old world recipes in her new world kitchen. She was a twentieth century immigrant and her name was Caterina. I became an American version of her and was named, out of love, respect and tradition, Catherine.

Grandma Tripolino, or "Nonna" as she would have been called, was a link to my Sicilian heritage and the Greenbush neighborhood where she lived. I was reminded by her black-clothed friends how much I looked like her. One day I realized how deeply I loved her without having known her and an obsession blossomed for the woman known as 'Donna Caterina.'

From tales shared, I learned about other grandmothers who lived in cold water flats, unheated apartments, bungalows and two-story homes. With nary a complaint of work that never ended, they lived side-by-side in harmony with old friends from their villages, and new friends who chatted in different languages over backyard fences while hanging out clothes, chasing chickens or plucking from gardens the fruit of their labor.

Before the stories ended, all the grandmothers of Greenbush had secured a place in my heart. They were kind and generous women whose breasts became soft pillows for their grandchildren. Although intense for their own, they opened their hearts to others, being cautious that no harm came to the other precious children of the neighborhood. If illnesses occurred in neighboring households, they sat bedside through the night.

"...we may have been from different ethnic groups, but we were all alike. We thought alike. We respected each other. And when someone was in need, everyone helped. We lived in the same block as the Caravello family. We were Jewish. They were Sicilians. I'll never forget the day little Jimmy Caravello was mauled by a polar bear at the Vilas Park Zoo. He was in serious condition and needed blood. By the time I got to the hospital, there was a line extending a full two blocks from the hospital with people from our Greenbush neighborhood. It didn't matter what religion we were, where we emigrated from, or what the color of our skin was. Each was there to give Jimmy the greatest gift we could...life from our own bodies. But despite our offerings and silent prayers, Jimmy died. It was like losing a member of our own family. Togetherness. That's what the old neighborhood was all about."
                                                            Sam Onheiber

Jimmy had become everyone's child and, when he died, people wept in unison. Togetherness was a mere fragment, however vital, of the Greenbush neighborhood each family called 'home.' Bordered by Park and Regent streets and West Washington Avenue, every ingredient, large and small, became a piece that snugly fit the design of Madison's first melting pot.

"...everybody was poor. We were a neighborhood of Italians, Jews, Irish and a few Blacks. We all got along. The kids all worked–they sold newspapers, ushered and worked at the ball games. Kids didn't have time to get into trouble..." Rachel Sweet Dutch

Affectionately referred to as the "Bush," the Greenbush settlement emerged from the dampness of a swampy plat to become a delight of grapevines, vegetable gardens, fruit trees, flowers, and aromas that drifted from open kitchen windows, through backyards and around corners where porches welcomed everyone and doors were never locked.

"...you want Stanley's fried chicken recipe? I don't have that. But what about spaghetti sauce? My mother-in-law made the best sauce in the neighborhood. She learned how from Felicia Pullara, her next door neighbor..." Dimetra Taliaferro Shivers

When Neighborhood House opened its doors on S. Park Street, civic-minded Madisonians became overnight guides to our grandmothers who questioned their new style of survival. Later, when its location changed to a West Washington Avenue furniture store-turned-community meeting hall, another plateau was reached by offering them a blueprint of America to study for citizenship status and their right to vote.

"....my mother did a little sewing for a few extra dollars that helped to bolster the barely adequate income from my father's job at the Roundhouse. Miss Braxton of the Neighborhood House saw to it that her friends brought some work to Ma. Many times my mother had opportunities to work outside of the home at some retail store or at someone's home doing many types of chores. But Father would not hear of it. It was still too 'early' in the century for such 'liberation' of the Italian woman..." Santo Zaccone

Greenbush was not where I was raised, but where my father and grandparents settled in 1911. Yet, in my heart, I knew I belonged there. I thrived on reflections of the past, and in my mind my roots became as deeply imbedded as those who claimed residences there. The aroma and treasures of my grandmother's kitchen on Gwinnette Court were meant to be remembered for life and my quest to capture what I could, through foods, began.

"...any visit, even unexpected, brought forth coffee (the best china for special guests, a sign of rispetto), a carafe of muscatel, port or marsala, and a tin or plate of homemade cookies–fig-filled cucidati, sweet seeded biscotti or, best of all, creamy filled cannoli. Fidi, famigghia, e un po' per manciari...faith, family and a little something to eat..." Father Charles Fiore

The adage, "beauty is in the eyes of the beholder," has never before resounded with such vigor as in recent years. Second, third and fourth generations thirst to make connections with the past when grandparents boasted of American citizenship, yet practiced Old World culture in the confines of their dwellings in an enclave of security.

"...an average day for Grandma included time to sit outside on the top step of the open stairway to the second floor sunroom at the back of the house. She enjoyed those moments for the warmth of the sun and health-giving benefits she believed this gave to her. I still see her there...with her homemade crocheted wine-colored triangular shawl around her shoulders...face tilted up to the sun, eyes closed, smiling, peaceful. On Fridays, with her head covered, she'd light the Sabbath candles before sundown. As she'd say the blessing, her arms would move gracefully over the challah and candles..." Sherry Lewis Wink

When we return to the memory of our grandmothers, we see dusty upstairs attics where things were stored in old trunks and boxes and basements where bread was baked on hot summer days and served in the coolness of its depths at suppertime. We feel intricate needlework that covered dining room tables, beds, davenport arms, and end tables where vases, statues and pictures of loved ones rested. We remember bed linens draped from second floor windows to air in the crispness of the early mornings, and smell the fragrance of hand-scrubbed floors covered with newspapers to protect them until company arrived. We savor memories of kitchens where kettles filled with soups and sauces were stirred with long-handled wooden spoons, and ovens were warm to the touch with nourishment for the family and anyone else who happened to stop by at the last moment. We think of freshly squeezed lemonade to pack in picnic baskets carried to nearby parks, rolling pins that created flaky-crusted pies to cool on window sills, and balmy evenings when friends and neighbors gathered on front porches and talked until it was time to climb the stairs to bedrooms where seeds were planted for new generations.

Greenbush, in all of its glory, was a 52-acre plat comprised of ten blocks that formed a triangular shaped neighborhood. The area didn't expand as neighborhoods do today. Instead, the heartbeat of the "Bush" remained confined within the streets of its periphery. When the enclave was razed during an urban renewal project in the 1960s, residents were scattered throughout the city, leaving behind only memories and the roots of grapevines hidden deep beneath the surface of the neighborhood our grandmothers so loved...

**Greenbush...
remembered**

"Memories are, in many ways,
who we are.
Without them we literally don't
know ourselves."

Professor of Psychology Joseph Hellige
University of Southern California

Margarita Intravaia

© Leah Intravaia Younker 1995

sketch by Leah Intravaia Younker

Welcome to the formative years of the
old Greenbush neighborhood when
mothers were wrapped in aprons and deep pockets
held sweet secrets for little ones...

1

Birthplace:	Piana degli Albanesi, Sicily
Parents:	Mateo Coronna and Cologera (Cascio) Coronna Salaparuta, Sicily
Siblings:	Joseph, Charles, Antonino, Antonina, Rose, Phillip, Mattew, Mary, Mathew
Spouse:	Ignatius Accardo Salaparuta, Sicily
Wedding:	Rockford, Illinois
Children:	Kathleen and Peter

Antonina Coronna Accardo
April 24, 1905 – August 18, 1990

Antonina and Ignatius Accardo resided at 213 S. Park Street in a small two-story house with a porch facing the street. Always fragrant with the aroma of homemade bread, the kitchen was large, bright, and cheerful.

"Nonna Accardo was everyone's picture of the 'quintessential' Sicilian grandmother. She was short, well-built, had large green eyes, and gray hair wrapped in a bun. Although she loved to cook, she loved even more to watch you eat the food she prepared. Her homemade pasta was smooth as velvet to the tongue. I can still see her hands patting out bread dough to fry and roll in sugar for us to eat while she baked the rest of the dough. We never ate 'fancy' at Nonna's house, but everything tasted so good. Everything seemed to be eaten with gusto. Bread, pasta, cheese. After dinner there were nuts and fruit. As kids, we were served biscotti and coffee, just like the grownups. Sunday was pasta-on-the-board day with noodles placed on wooden boards supported by the table. She'd pour sauce over the pasta, then garnish everything with freshly snipped basil. During the holidays the kitchen was filled with lots of chatter as her friends gathered to make cucidati. She relaxed in the evening, after supper, sipping coffee with milk while playing solitaire."

Carl Welke, grandson
(son of Kathleen Accardo Welke)

Nonna Accardo's Bread

"I remember the way she cut bread...by holding it close to her chest."

5 pounds of flour, sifted
2 tablespoons salt
2 tablespoons sugar
1/2 cup corn oil
2 eggs
2 ounces cake yeast
Warm milk and
sesame seeds for topping

Dissolve yeast in warm water and allow to form a sponge. Combine flour, sugar and salt in large pan and make a well in the center; break egg in well. Add oil and yeast, adding water as needed. Knead until all flour is picked up without sticking to pan. When dough has been kneaded to a silky consistency, oil bottom of pan. Place dough in pan and cover. Allow to rise in warm place for 1 hour. Punch down and let rise another hour. Cut dough and place in oiled pans and allow to rise again. Wash tops with warm milk and sprinkle with seeds. Bake at 350 degrees for 1 hour or until golden.

Note: Place pan of water in oven while bread is baking to make crust crisp.

Birthplace: Piana degli Albanesi, Sicily

Parents: Frank and Josephine (Mandala) Salerno

Siblings: George, Tony, Lawrence, and Conchera

Spouse: Philip Barbato
Piana degli Albanesi, Sicily

Wedding: July 31, 1916, Madison, Wisconsin

Children: Grace, 1920, and Josephine, 1923

Rose Salerno Barbato
July 10, 1902 –

*R*ose and Philip Barbato had many addresses in the Greenbush neighborhood. The 14 N. Park Street location they moved to in 1920 is remembered with great fondness. The house, situated on a corner lot, is described by family as being very large. Besides having a living room, dining room and kitchen on first floor, they also enjoyed a walk-in pantry, and screened porch where Grace and Josephine slept when summer evenings became unbearably warm. Three bedrooms and a bath occupied second floor. Rose Barbato's family was extremely important to her. While her father made his home with the Barbato family, Rose became a special grandmother to the next generation, grandson, Joe Germono, and granddaughter, Rosanne.

"Mom is one of few of her generation from the Greenbush neighborhood who drove a car. I can still see her behind the wheel of our big Buick. Her brother, Lawrence, was a well-known singer and staff member at WGN in Chicago. Oftentimes, he would call Mom at 10 p.m. to tell her he was bringing celebrities to our house for a 'late' spaghetti dinner. Arrival time was usually about one or two in the morning. She'd call Mr. Reda who would immediately leave his house to open his store and cut the meat she needed. Ingredients for sauce was always available as she canned 18 bushels or more of tomatoes each year. When company arrived they'd all sit down to eat until the sun came up. They were good times...She continued to make bread until she fell about two years ago. She relies on a walker now, but is good at advising me when I try my hand at duplicating some of the delicious food she used to prepare."

Josephine Barbato Petratta, daughter

Rose's Veal Steak

"One of her favorite meals prepared for those early morning gatherings..."

1 pound of veal steak
1 egg, beaten
Bread crumbs, seasoned with salt, pepper,
      Parmesan cheese, garlic powder, and parsley
1 15-ounce can of peas, drained
Spaghetti sauce

Dip veal in egg, then in crumb mixture. Brown on both sides in oil and put on paper towel to drain off excess oil. Using a 2 quart casserole, layer ingredients in this order; sauce, veal, then peas. Repeat, remembering to finish with sauce for the top. Bake covered at 350 degrees for 45 minutes. This course would be served with a tossed salad and homemade bread. Fresh fruit was served following the meal.

Birthplace: Houma, Louisiana

Parents: Peter Savone and Calogera (LaBella) Savone, Salaparuta, Sicily

Siblings: Sarah, Nick, Carl, Tony, Sam, and Joe

Spouse: Joseph Barber, Castelvegrano, Sicily

Wedding: February 10, 1917 St. Joseph's Catholic Church, Madison, Wisconsin

Children: Rose, 1919; Gasper, 1921; Charlotte, 1923; Peter, 1925; Angeline, 1932

Mary Annette Savone Barber
January 6, 1898 – October 22, 1995

When Mary Barber was three, her family left the New Orleans area and sugar cane plantation employment to settle in Streeter, Illinois. A few years later, they moved to Madison where her father would build a home at 714 Milton St. When she was 18, the family moved to a farm near Pittsville. Joseph Barber had fallen in love with Mary and often visited the Savone family until a marriage proposal could be arranged. After a two month engagement, the couple married and settled in the Greenbush neighborhood.

Civic issues were of great importance to Mary Barber. She and four others established a PTA at the newly built St. Joseph's School, 12 S. Park St. Instrumental in founding other school and church societies, Mary devoted herself to the Civic League to raise money for university scholarships for Italian students. When New York-based UNICO came to Madison, the two groups merged. She also chaired Red Cross/Red Feather in her district for eight years before it became part of United Way. When the Italian-American Women's Mutual Aid Society and the Sicilian Women's Bersagliere Club founded in 1934, Mary joined forces and later served as President, as well as other offices. Her efforts were recognized in 1979 when Madison's Italian community presented her with the Columbian of the Year Award.

"After my grandparents died and the language no longer was used on a daily basis, my mother enrolled at the University of Wisconsin to brush up on her Italian language skills to better serve the community. As chairperson, she was instrumental in helping St. Joseph's parish raise money to send Father Neault to Rome for his Silver Jubilee. When Bishop O'Connor was invited to attend the ham dinner in the church hall, his response was 'only if Italian food is served.' The menu changed immediately. Father Neault returned from Rome with an autographed picture of Pope Pius XII which became one of her most valued possessions. It seemed that everything she did was a major accomplishment."

Rose Barber Edwards, daughter

Nucatole

"This pop-up cookie recipe belonged to my mother and brings back wonderful memories..."

6 eggs
2 pounds of powdered sugar
1/2 teaspoon baking powder
2 teaspoons vanilla, or almond extract
5 cups flour, or 4 1/2 cups flour plus 1/2 cup very finely chopped almonds that resemble flour

Beat eggs at high speed until light and fluffy. Add powdered sugar and flavoring and beat. Add flour and mix. You may have to use fingers to mix. Let stand 30 minutes, or more. Roll and shape into 1/2-inch logs and cut, or shape into balls. Place on greased cookie sheet. Let rise at least 2 hours. Bake 12-15 minutes. Can use a small size 60 scoop if making small balls. Divide recipe to make half the amount.

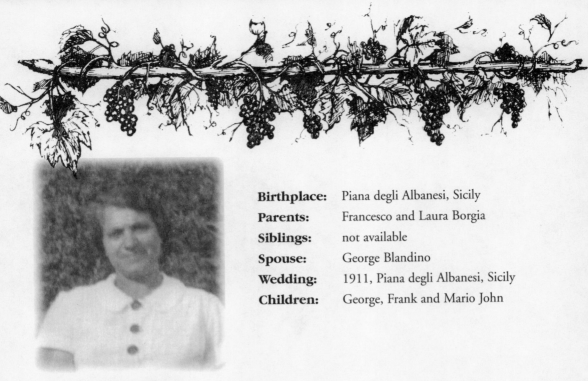

Birthplace:	Piana degli Albanesi, Sicily
Parents:	Francesco and Laura Borgia
Siblings:	not available
Spouse:	George Blandino
Wedding:	1911, Piana degli Albanesi, Sicily
Children:	George, Frank and Mario John

Chinia Borgia Blandino
March 16, 1889 – November 21, 1982

George and Chinia (Frances), and their son, George, arrived in this country in 1921. They lived on N. Murray Street before moving a few blocks away to Spring Street. When the University of Wisconsin purchased the home many years later, Frances, by then a widow, moved to Braxton Apartments near Park and Regent streets. At age 70, Frances Blandino returned to her village in Sicily for a two-month visit.

"Some of our favorite memories revolve around food and her expertise in making the homemade pasta we referred to as lasagna. She'd roll out two huge sheets of dough using a long wooden roller, then fold it into a 2-inch strip. Using her thumb as a guide, she quickly cut the dough into long strips, laying each out to dry and cook later to serve with sauce 'on the board.' We always worried that she would cut her finger when slicing it as fast as she did. She was just as quick with crochet needles. What she completed was so beautifully done that three generations of Blandino's still enjoy the treasures in their own homes."

Mrs. Frank (Lila) Blandino, daughter-in-law

Baked Pasta Milanesa

"...some of our favorite memories revolve around food..."

1/4 cup chopped onions
1 garlic clove, chopped fine
2 tablespoons olive oil
26 ounces of spaghetti sauce with basil
1 8 1/2-ounce can of pasta con sarde
1 teaspoon sugar
1 pound of spaghetti
Grated Parmesan cheese
2 tablespoons bread crumbs
1 teaspoon butter or margarine
1/4 teaspoon sugar

In saucepan, sauté onions and garlic in oil; add your own homemade spaghetti sauce, or a jar of what is listed in the ingredients above, and simmer about 45 minutes. Stir occasionally; add sugar about 5 minutes before turning off heat. Cook spaghetti, drain and pour back into same pan. Combine can of pasta con sarde with spaghetti, adding about 1/2 the spaghetti sauce. Mix well and put in lightly greased 9 by 13-inch baking pan. Add remaining sauce making certain a good portion spreads into the spaghetti. Sprinkle grated Parmesan cheese over top. Melt butter or margarine on low heat and add bread crumbs, stirring until lightly brown. Add sugar and stir. Sprinkle over pasta Milanesa. Cover with aluminum foil and bake 30 minutes at 350 degrees. Serves 4 to 6.

Birthplace: San Cipirello, Sicily

Parents: Salvatore and Grazia (Orlando) Manino

Siblings: Sam, Tony, John, Joe, Lebonio, Phillipo, and Nicolo

Spouse: Antonio Bonanno, San Giuseppe Iato, Sicily

Wedding: 1907, San Cipirello, Sicily

Children: Mary, 1913; Sam, 1915; Grace, 1917; Ann, 1920; Tony, 1925; and Sophie, 1932. (Two others died in infancy.)

Antonina (Annie) Manino Bonanno
September 12, 1890 – June 4, 1980

Annie and Antonio Bonanno settled in Madison in a three-story house at 713 Milton Street. Because basements were necessities to Italian families, Antonino installed radiators on the basement ceiling and laid a wooden floor to cover with linoleum for Annie's summer kitchen. It was where the family gathered for meals during warm weather, and where fruits and vegetables were preserved at the end of the growing season. Partitioned was an area where wine was made with a grape press imbedded in concrete. A rack held two wooden barrels for wine. Large sacks of flour and sugar were also stored in the basement with cases of macaroni, canned tomatoes, peaches, caponatina, and crocks of peppers, tomato paste and olives. Snow apples filled other barrels, while potatoes and onions were stored in bins.

"A normal day for Grandma began about 5:30 in the morning. After making breakfast and packing lunches for everyone, she'd concentrate on housework and what to prepare for supper. She loved to cook and bake and always had food on hand for anyone who was hungry. If something needed fixing, she'd hire a handyman, then pay him with food, grandpa's wine, and a little cash. In her spare time, she'd crochet. There were crocheted curtains on the front door, doilies on the davenport, on every table, on her piano, and even covering her shiny brass bed. All were starched. My mom's job was to unsnarl the tassels with a comb – a chore she disliked. When four o'clock arrived, Grandma washed up with a bar of Jap Rose soap purchased at Lucky Pharmacy, slipped on a clean housedress, then waited at the window for Grandpa to walk home from his job at Gisholt Company. Just as he'd round the corner, the burner was turned on under the pasta kettle, and a quart of cold orange pop was opened as a refresher after a hard day of work. By the time he washed up, the table was set and the family sat down together for supper."

Sandra Boland Hunter, granddaughter

Grandma Bonanno's Italian Fig Cookies

"For 37 years, Annie Bonanno gave thanks to St. Joseph for curing her husband of a life-threatening illness. Each March 19th, an altar was prepared in her home with statues, tapestries and food, some of which was prepared weeks in advance, like fig cookies by the bushel."

Dough:

4 1/2 cups flour

1 1/2 tablespoons baking powder

1/4 teaspoon salt

1 cup sugar

2 cups margarine, room temperature

1 teaspoon vanilla

3 eggs

1/4 cup milk

Make five recipes of dough for 12 rings of dried figs. Mix flour, baking powder and salt and set aside. In another bowl, mix sugar, margarine and vanilla; cream well. Combine and work both mixtures until crumbly, like pie dough. With your hands, add milk and eggs to batter, being careful not to overmix. Refrigerate overnight. Roll out on lightly floured surface. Add filling, cut, trim, then bake at 350 degrees for 15 to 20 minutes, or until golden. Frost and sprinkle with decoration while cookies are still warm.

Filling:

4 large navel oranges

3 teaspoons cinnamon

2 quarts honey

12 rings of figs, ground

3 12-ounce packages Hershey milk chocolate chips, finely chopped or ground

40 ounces of slivered almonds, toasted, cooled, and chopped

Peel oranges, removing white pith from rind. Broil peel, watching carefully, until rind gets brown and rock hard. Cool and grind. Mix with honey. Mix together all ingredients and let sit for a few days before baking. Note: To mix fig filling, divide ground figs evenly in two large containers. Divide and add almonds, chocolate, honey with cinnamon and orange peel. Mix thoroughly by hand.

Frosting:

Make 5 recipes for entire cookie recipe

3 egg whites

3 cups powdered sugar

1-2 teaspoons of lemon juice, or to taste

Whip egg whites until stiff. Add powdered sugar and lemon juice. Whip until glossy. Make icing, one batch at a time, as it hardens quickly.

Birthplace: Piana degli Albanesi, Sicily

Parents: John and Josephine (Guidera) Licali, Piana degli Albanesi, Sicily

Siblings: Dominic, Elizabeth, George, Victoria and Ninfa

Spouse: Giuseppe Brashi, Piana degli Albanesi, Sicily

Wedding: June 1908, Madison, Wisconsin

Children: Sarah, 1906; Vito, 1908; Josephine, 1912; John, 1915; Katherine, 1917; Dominic, 1919; Georgina, 1922; Elizabeth, 1924; and Ann 1926

Maria Licali Brashi
December 8, 1885 – August 3, 1979

After her father died, Maria and her sisters accompanied their mother to New Orleans to join Dominic and George who were working the sugar cane fields. Later, George would leave New Orleans for Madison to join village friends and family already settled there. Leaving Dominic in New Orleans, the rest of the family followed and settled at 824 Regent St. In 1908, Maria married Giuseppe Brashi. The newlyweds lived at 826 Regent St. until moving to a place of their own at 1029 S. Park St. in a small two-story stucco, three bedroom house. Because the kitchen was small with no counter space, the table was used to prepare food served in the dining room. When the children had grown and left home, the upstairs was converted to an apartment. Many fruit trees grew in the backyard, including a lemon tree that found an opening to grow through the wooden boards of the back porch floor. A massive grapevine extended from the house to the back lot line. Although she relaxed by crocheting, Maria also loved listening to Stella Dallas on the radio.

"A cherished recollection is of my mother making homemade noodles. It amazed me how uniform each piece was considering how fast she worked. Every Sunday when we'd sit around the board and eat pasta with homemade sauce and some of the 12 loaves of bread baked each week. She was also my best friend. If any of us had a problem, she'd sit down and listen. By the time the conversation ended, the crisis was over. She treated everyone like that. She was the grandest lady I have ever known."

Josephine Brashi Blankenheim, daughter

"My Nonna and Nonni had country property out toward Oregon where they planted fava beans. When it was time to harvest and shell the beans, their 'cronies' were invited to the house. They'd spend the afternoon sitting together in the backyard, eating fava and sipping homemade red wine."

Lucy Cuccia Borcherding, granddaughter
(daughter of Katherine)

Seasoned Fava Beans

"Nonna boiled and seasoned any leftover fava to serve alone, or with pasta, for supper..."

1 pound dried fava beans, soaked overnight
3 tablespoons good quality olive oil
1 small onion
Salt and freshly ground black pepper to taste
1/3 cup water
Chopped fresh parsley for garnish

Shell soaked fava beans and wash them in cold water. Heat oil in a large heavy pot and sauté onion until golden. Add beans and stir until coated with oil. Add salt and pepper to taste. Add the 1/3 cup of water and stir. Cover pot and simmer over low heat until beans are soft and the water has evaporated. Sprinkle with parsley and serve immediately as an appetizer or a side dish.

Birthplace:	Castelvetrano, Sicily
Parents:	Pietro and Caterina (Bellafiori) Fumusa
Siblings:	Saverio, James, Joseph, and Mark
Spouse:	Joseph Brusca, Passo de Rigano, Sicily
Wedding:	1922, St. Joseph's Catholic Church, Madison, Wisconsin
Children:	Agostino, 1923; Joseph, 1925.

Laura Fumusa Brusca
January 4, 1900 – February 11, 1975

Home for the Brusca family in the Greenbush neighborhood meant Park Street, Desmond Court, and 14 N. Mills Street. They were simple dwellings with bare essentials during very difficult times. After Agostino's death, Laura's husband tragically lost his life. Five months later, she gave birth to another son, Joseph. Because she had not totally recovered from a previous illness, Laura and the baby moved in with her mother who was barely existing on a $50.00 check received monthly after her brother Mark, was killed in France where he served in the military during World War I.

"Thanks to relatives and Mr. Balsamo, we managed. Rent was $15.00 a month with everything furnished. Mr. Balsamo let us have all we could eat from his garden. My mother canned sauce, peaches, pears, apples and anything else available during the growing season. We never ate store purchased bread. My grandmother and mother made the best bread I have ever eaten. Life was very hard and lonely for my mother. She never remarried, yet with the help of friends and relatives, somehow we made it."

Joseph Brusca, son

Hard Crust Sicilian Bread

"You make the sign of the cross, then let it rise for two hours."

2 packages dry yeast (not self-rising)
1 teaspoon sugar
1 egg
1 tablespoon olive oil
2 teaspoons salt
3 1/2 cups warm water
12 cups of Robin Hood flour
1 egg, beaten for top
Sesame seeds

Dissolve yeast in 1/2 cup of warm water and 1 teaspoon sugar. Let stand 10 minutes. Beat one egg, 1 tablespoon olive oil, and 2 teaspoons of salt and put in 3 1/2 cups of warm water; mix. Make a well in 12 cups of flour and add all ingredients. Mix well and knead for 10 minutes. Grease a large bowl with a small amount of olive oil. Cover with a blanket or two. Make the sign of the cross and let it rise for 2 hours. After 2 hours, knead it again and let rise for another hour. Grease 6 small or 3 large bread pans. Braid dough before brushing with 1 beaten egg. Sprinkle with sesame seeds. Let stand for 30 minutes. Bake in oven for 1 hour and 15 minutes at 375 degrees. For extra hard crust, during the last 20 minutes, keep turning bread in pans.

Note: If making pizza dough, allow to rise only once.

Birthplace:	San Giuseppe Iato, Sicily
Parents:	Philip and Rosetta (Napoli) Cassata
	Grandparents: Salvatore and Catherine
	Consiglio, Favarotta, Sicily
Siblings:	John, Josephine, Marietta, and Joseph
Spouse:	Joseph Canepa
Wedding:	February 20, 1909
	San Giuseppe Iato, Sicily
Children:	Theodore, Philip, Anthony, Christopher,
	and John

Caterina "Titina" Cassata Canepa
January 31, 1893 – December 20, 1967

Although she was beautiful as well as being a talented piano and mandolin player, Caterina Napoli was also very religious and entered the convent in San Giuseppe Iato at a young age with the intent to become a nun. Joseph Canepa left the same village, arriving in New York when he was 15 years old. After living in Dodgeville, New York, he returned to his village in Sicily to claim the woman his father had arranged for him to marry. Caterina's plans to become a nun ended on the day she turned 16. Joseph Canepa, a young man she had never met, took her from the convent to be his wife. They left for New York immediately after the wedding, lived in Dodgeville, celebrated the birth of their first son, Theodore, then returned to Sicily where Anthony was born. The second time they sailed to this country, they went directly to Madison and settled in the Greenbush neighborhood in a three-story house on the corner at 29 S. Murray Street. The Canepa's clothing and shoe store occupied the first floor of the building. Living quarters, including two kitchens, were established on second and third floors. Caterina, also known as "Titina," kept herself busy as a homemaker, tending the store with her husband, and as a member of the Italian Women's Club, the Bersagliere, and Madison Catholic Women. She enjoyed directing plays at St. Joseph's Church on S. Park Street. Life was very good for the Canepa family .

"My mother would tell us of her aristocratic grandparents, the Napolis, who owned many farms and much property in Sicily. Onofrio Napoli had received a university education. With such a background, it is no surprise that my mother was refined. She was a lovely and beautiful person. Aside from all the things she did for us, helping in the store, and being an active member in various organizations, she loved planning picnics at Gay's Woods for Italian students enrolled at the University of Wisconsin."

Ted T. Canepa, son

Grandma Canepa's Sesame Seed Cookies

*"...she loved planning picnics at Gay's Woods for Italian students
enrolled at the University of Wisconsin."*

2/3 cup margarine
1 cup sugar
3 eggs
1 teaspoon vanilla
4 cups flour
1 teaspoon baking powder
1/2 teaspoon salt
Sesame seeds

Cream well margarine and sugar. Add eggs, one at a time, beating well. Add vanilla, then dry ingredient mixture and beat until smooth and workable. If necessary, add more flour if dough is sticky. Cut dough in pieces and roll into 1/2-inch rope. Roll rope in sesame seeds and cut into 1 1/2 by 2-inches and place each piece on a cookie sheet. Bake at 375 degrees for 12 to 15 minutes.

Birthplace:	Piana degli Albanesi, Sicily
Parents:	Tomasso and Giuseppina (Giuseppe) Riolo
Siblings:	Frank, Matteo, and Antonina
Spouse:	George Capaci, Piana degli Albanesi, Sicily
Wedding:	April 21, 1912, Piana degli Albanesi, Sicily
Children:	Maria, 1913; Sarah, 1917; Mary 1919; Joseph, 1920; Josephine, 1925

Leanora Riolo Capaci
July 7, 1894 – December 11, 1988

Leanora and George Capaci arrived in the United States in 1914. They lived on University Avenue before moving to S. Park Street across from St. Joseph's Church. When George became ill, the family returned to their village in Sicily. When they moved back to Madison in 1924, they stayed at 923 Spring Street until 1929 at which time they moved to 1140 E. Lakeside Street near Olin Park. It is where they would remain until November 1935 when a situation they had no control of during the Depression forced foreclosure on their property.

"The six-room house in the swampy area across from Olin Park meant happiness for all of us. For 32 months my father dug ditches to drain water from the land while upgrading many other things on the property. By the time he finished, we had a wine and fruit cellar under both front and back porches. My mother was so happy. The garden was the size of a city block and among a variety of vegetables planted were 2600 tomato plants. When we applied for a restaurant permit to sell candy and ice cream in our front yard, my mother decided she'd like to serve spaghetti to anyone who just happened to stop by...hungry. Homemade wine was served with each dinner. People attending carnivals at the fairground became customers. One day an eviction notice was delivered. We never expected anything like that to happen, but it was a sign of the times and once again we had to move."

Sarah Curning and Josie Hagen, daughters

Sarah Curning's Sesame Seed Cookies

"I wonder how many bushels of these I have made through the years. Crispy and nutty-flavored, each bite is a reminder of the past."

1 1/2 pounds of flour
3/4 pound Crisco
3/4 pound sugar
4 tablespoons baking powder
4 eggs
1/4 teaspoon salt
3/4 cup milk
1/2 of a .125 fluid ounce bottle of anise flavored oil
　　or 1 small (1 fl. oz.) bottle anise extract
Sesame seeds

Mix together, roll in log, and cut in 2-inch pieces. Dip in additional beaten egg, then roll in seeds to coat. Bake on ungreased pan in 400 degree oven until dark golden brown.

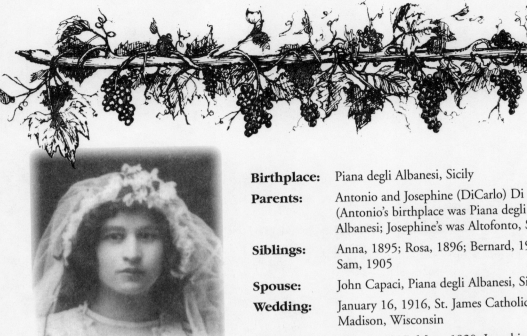

Birthplace:	Piana degli Albanesi, Sicily
Parents:	Antonio and Josephine (DiCarlo) Di Gregorio (Antonio's birthplace was Piana degli Albanesi; Josephine's was Altofonto, Sicily)
Siblings:	Anna, 1895; Rosa, 1896; Bernard, 1901; Sam, 1905
Spouse:	John Capaci, Piana degli Albanesi, Sicily
Wedding:	January 16, 1916, St. James Catholic Church, Madison, Wisconsin
Children:	George, 1917; Mary, 1920; Josephine, 1921; Nina, 1923; Margaret, 1924; Victoria, 1926; Ann, 1930; Rose, 1932; Jennie, 1934; Delores, 1937

Rose Di Gregorio Capaci
November 7, 1896 – October 15, 1973

After their wedding, Rose and John moved upstairs of her parents at 8 South Lake Street. As their family grew, larger living quarters were needed. John drew plans to build a home for his family and in March of 1927, moved to a new six-bedroom, two-bathroom house at 1025 S. Park St. When the family continued to grow, the basement was converted to a second kitchen furnished with a wood stove and a large table. Although Rose used her gas stove during the cold winter months, she also used the wood stove for added warmth. Her summer garden rewarded the family throughout the year with an ample supply of home canned food. When babies were born, it was at the house, with Dr. Colucci in attendance.

"If she had any spare time, it was enjoyed by crocheting or making rag rugs. Grandma was God's wonderful gift to our family. As one of her 25 grandchildren, I can attest to her lessons in sharing and appreciating the important things in life. Yet, her food preparation holds the most vivid memories for me. Every Sunday we gathered together as a family. This meant preparing huge quantities of food. Meatballs and sauce simmered all day making the house smell...delicious. And I remember how she made bread, covering each loaf before placing them in the back spare room to rise. Because she couldn't read or write very well, nothing was recorded. If I asked her how to make something, her response was 'with a pinch of this, and a pinch of that.' The meal I remember best was the chicken cacciatore she called something like 'chicken in lunk.' Another one we called 'brooma greesa.'"

Shirley Hilgers, granddaughter
(daughter of Josephine)

"Brooma Greesa"

"The meal I remember best was the chicken cacciatore she called something like 'chicken in lunk.' Another one we called 'brooma greesa.'"

1 bag of shell macaroni
1 pound of fresh ricotta cheese
Milk
Salt and pepper to taste
Garlic powder to taste

Boil macaroni as directed on package. While boiling pasta, mix cheese in a bowl with enough milk, salt, pepper and garlic powder to make a sauce. The amounts used should suit your personal taste for garlic and smoothness. Once it is mixed, pour over macaroni. Serve with garlic bread and a salad.

Birthplace:	Piana degli Albanesi, Sicily
Parents:	John and Josephine (Guidera) Licali
Siblings:	Dominic, George, Elizabeth, Victoria and Mary
Spouse:	Vito Capadona, Sr. Piana degli Albanesi, Sicily
Wedding:	May 29, 1913, Freeport, Illinois
Children:	Conchera, Vito, Jr., John, Joe ("Pino"), and George

Ninfa Licali Capadona
October 29, 1899 – September 20, 1995

*B*y the time the Greenbush neighborhood became victim to urban renewal in the 1960s, roots of the Capadona family were deeply imbedded on the corner of Park and Regent streets. Still referred to today by longtime Madisonians as "Spaghetti Corners," it had been the busy intersection of Highways 12, 13, 14 and 151. The Capadona three-story dwelling at 826 Regent Street not only was the family home, but also the location of Capadona's neighborhood grocery store. After Prohibition, it became "Bunky's," a tiny bar serving giant portions of Italian food prepared in the kitchen by Ninfa Capadona. She played an important roll in introducing authentic Old World flavors to Madisonians, as well as how the true Sicilian pizza should look and taste.

"My mother spent her days and evenings in the restaurant kitchen preparing and serving Italian specialities city residents couldn't seem to get enough of. She charged 35 cents for a spaghetti dinner. What a deal that was. After an hour spent there you'd have memories for a lifetime. I think the kitchen was her favorite place to be. In fact, I know it was."

Conchera "Connie" Pullara, daughter

Breaded Round Steak

"The corner was always alive with people. And so were our kitchens. It's where my mother was happiest. In the kitchen on the corner..."

1 pound round steak, cut in pieces
2 eggs
2 cups bread crumbs
1/2 cup grated Parmesan or Romano cheese
Flour
2 teaspoons salt
Parsley
Butter
Mushrooms, optional

Cut meat in any size pieces. Beat eggs in bowl, dip meat in eggs, then coat with bread mixture of crumbs, cheese, flour, salt, and parsley. Pat down. Brown in hot oil. Put in layers in a greased baking dish. Bake for 1 hour. Dot meat with butter. Adding mushrooms is optional.

Birthplace: Italy

Parents: Vito and Jennie (Bonino) Covernali

Siblings: Carlo, Mary, and Vito

Spouse: Antonio Cardarella, Italy

Wedding: 1912, St. Joseph's Catholic Church, Madison, Wisconsin

Children: Vito, 1913; Anthony, 1915; Frances, 1917; Peter, 1919; George, 1922; Carl, 1924; Albert, 1926; Mary Jane, 1929; Paul, 1931; Joseph, 1933; Angeline, 1936; Rose, 1938; Betty, 1943.

Anna Covernali Cardarella
May 17, 1899 – September 25, 1967

When Anna Covernali was thirteen years old, she and Antonio Cardarella married. All but the last two babies were born at home at 820 Milton St. with a midwife in attendance. Anna is described as a "saint." She was a homemaker who took one day at a time, managing with limited funds to feed her large family. A kind and generous wife, mother, and mother-in-law, Anna doted on family, taking great pleasure in the grandchildren who would complement her life. Radio and television was a form of entertainment, as was "Tweety-pie," a parakeet she managed to teach a few words to. When the Greenbush neighborhood was razed during the 1960s, Anna moved to 620 S. Mills Street.

"Papa Cardarella died on Thanksgiving Day. It was a very sad day for all of us. After that, Anna never celebrated the day again as a holiday."

Mrs. George (Lucille) Cardarella

"I will always remember seeing her cleaning burdock, or cardune, as she called it. She'd have to pick it before the farmers dug it up to prevent their cows from eating it. The farmers claimed it soured the cow's milk. Cardune and dandelion greens. Both were so tasty the way she prepared them. One day my mother came over to visit and Anna was preparing cardune. When it was ready to eat, my mother tasted it. She remarked how delicious it was. I told her that it was the "terrible weed" she used to dig up. She couldn't believe it. Another favorite recipe was pasta e piselli, a meatball, potato and pea combination. Simply delicious, but I could never get it to taste the same."

Mrs. Vito (Virginia) Cardarella

Mama C's Spaghetti Sauce and Meatballs

"Everything she made was delicious. Breaded eggplant, olive salad, a meal of meatballs, potatoes and peas, and of course, spaghetti and meatballs."

1 large jar of homemade tomato sauce
2 cans tomato paste
1 garlic clove
Salt to taste
1 scant tablespoon sugar (to cut the acidity)

Mix tomato sauce and paste with equal parts of water in a heavy kettle. Drop in garlic clove. Salt to taste and add sugar. Simmer slowly, stirring occasionally. Remove garlic clove before serving.

Meatballs:
1 1/2 pound ground beef
2 eggs
1/2 cup finely ground bread, or saltine soda crackers
1/4 teaspoon garlic powder
1/4 teaspoon onion powder
Salt to taste
Grated Parmesan cheese, optional

Mix together and shape into firm meatballs. Drop in hot spaghetti sauce without browning first. Meatballs will be tender and keep their shape better. Prepare your favorite pasta. When done, rinse in colander with water to remove starch. Serve spaghetti, meatballs and sauce with grated Parmesan, if desired.

Birthplace:	Piana degli Albanesi, Sicily
Parents:	Joseph and Josephine (Piediscalizi) Matranga
Siblings:	not available
Spouse:	Pietro Ciulla, Piana degli Albanesi, Sicily
Wedding:	1901, S. Demetrio Ni, Piana degli Albanesi, Sicily
Children:	Giacino, Odigitria (Beatrice), Joseph and Pietro

Francesca Matranga Ciulla
April 9, 1876 – November 13, 1957

$\mathcal{P}$ietro "Peter" Ciulla came to this country in 1910, lived in Montana, then moved to Wisconsin. Francesca arrived in Madison in 1919. The hardship and loneliness they endured during their separation was typical of what other immigrants experienced. Money was sent home each month, but two wars interfered with travel plans for Francesca and her mother. When she arrived here, they moved into a two-story, three bedroom home at 36 S. Brooks Street. After Pietro died, Francesca moved to an apartment above Corona's Market on the corner of S. Murray and Regent streets.

"She was such a tiny woman,...so tiny that you couldn't see her in her garden unless she wore a bandanna. Her Victory garden was located off Park Street and it was where she spent most of her time. Marigolds and zinnias were her favorite flowers and complemented all the vegetables she grew with their colorful blossoms. I remember a fish salad she used to make with green olives, lemon and parsley. It was very special, but since nothing was ever written down, I've never been able to duplicate it. The sesame bread she made was shaped into round loaves, and veal, breaded and fried, was served with a variety of vegetables from the garden."

Lorita Gooch Eagle, granddaughter

Seafood Salad
Insalata di Gamberi e Pettine

"This is the closest recipe I have found to what is remembered of her fish salad"

> 1 teaspoon salt
> 1 pound medium shrimp, shelled and deveined
> 1 teaspoon salt
> 1 pound bay scallops, thoroughly washed to remove sand
> 1 1/2 cups thinly sliced celery, strings removed
> 1/2 cup medium-size pimiento-stuffed green olives
>   (about 18), well-drained & halved
> 1 large head romaine lettuce (1 1/2 pounds-garnish)

In 4-quart pot, bring 2 quarts of water to boil; add 1 teaspoon salt. Place shrimp in pot and cover. As soon as water returns to boil, uncover and cook shrimp until they are pink—about 2 minutes, but do not overcook or shrimp will be tough. Drain in strainer; rinse under cold water and blot dry with paper toweling. In a 10-inch skillet, bring 2 cups water to a boil and add 1 teaspoon salt. Place scallops in pan in a single layer and cover. As soon as water returns to boil, uncover and cook scallops 1 minute. Transfer to strainer; rinse in cold water, drain well and blot dry with paper toweling.

Two hours in advance of serving: Combine shrimp, scallops, celery, olives in a large bowl. Discard the outer leaves of romaine lettuce which are bruised. Trim tough bottom ends and wash several times in cold water to remove sand. Spin dry in a salad spinner or blot dry with paper toweling. Set aside.

Dressing:

1/2 cup olive oil	1 teaspoon salt
1 tablespoon grated lemon rind	1/2 teaspoon freshly milled white pepper
1/4 cup fresh lemon juice	3 tablespoons minced Italian parsley leaves
1/2 teaspoon sugar	3 tablespoons snipped chives

In a small bowl, combine all ingredients and mix well with a wire whisk or food processor fitted with a metal blade. Pour dressing over seafood; cover with plastic wrap and refrigerate for two hours (do not marinate any longer or seafood will become soggy). To serve, arrange lettuce leaves around edge of a larger platter. Toss seafood salad again and transfer to center of platter. Serve immediately.

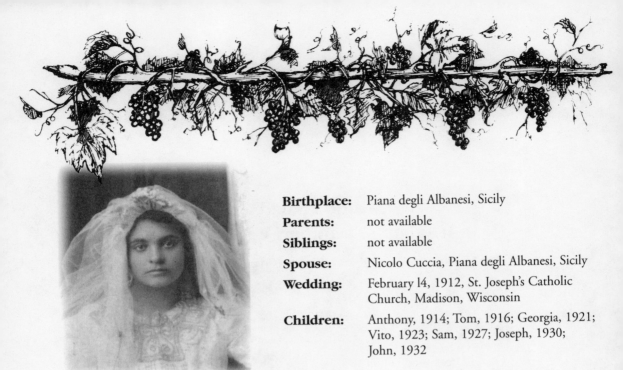

Birthplace: Piana degli Albanesi, Sicily

Parents: not available

Siblings: not available

Spouse: Nicolo Cuccia, Piana degli Albanesi, Sicily

Wedding: February 14, 1912, St. Joseph's Catholic Church, Madison, Wisconsin

Children: Anthony, 1914; Tom, 1916; Georgia, 1921; Vito, 1923; Sam, 1927; Joseph, 1930; John, 1932

Frances Stassi Cuccia
November 9, 1884 – June, 1971

*T*heir addresses in the "Bush," 826 Regent Street, 7 S. Park Street, 707 and 809 Milton Street, became gathering places for the children. Among the many other special things in Frances Cuccia's life, such as the movies, and later, television, included the orange and lemon trees that grew from seed in the backyard. After the neighborhood was razed, she would become one of the first residents to move into the Braxton Apartments.

"She was a wonderful person. Although each day seemed to be filled with chores for my mother-in-law, she always saved time in the afternoon to visit with neighbors, friends and relatives. For each birthday, or any other family celebration, everyone was invited to her house. Everything she made was delicious. Oven-baked chicken, veal, fried bread, thick pizza with anchovies, soup and pasta. The house always smelled good. Because my mother passed away when I was only 13, my mother-in-law taught me about house cleaning and, of course, how to cook. This was one of her favorites."

Mrs. Joseph (Shirley) Cuccia

Chicken and Beef with Pasta Soup

*"When I married her son in 1956, she became the mother I lost when I was young.
She taught me how to do everything. My memories of her are very special.
This was one of her favorites."*

1 chicken, cut up
1 small 2-3 pound pot roast
1 large onion
2 cups chopped celery, or 6 stalks, chopped
10 carrots, or 2 1/2 cups chopped carrots
1 large can of tomatoes
1 1/2 teaspoon sweet basil
1 teaspoon oregano
1 teaspoon garlic powder, or to taste
1 tablespoon dry parsley, or half the amount if using
    fresh parsley
2 cups macaroni, or acini di Pepe, cooked,
    amount to your liking
Grated Parmesan or Romano cheese

In large stockpot, cover chicken and roast with water. Add all the ingredients, except pasta, and cook until meat is tender. Remove skin and bones. Return meat to broth and vegetables. Add pasta: heat thoroughly. Serve with grated Parmesan or Romano cheese.

Birthplace: Piana degli Albanesi, Sicily

Parents: Sam and Anna (Buccola) Fiorenza

Siblings: Giuseppe, Giovanbattista, Mercurio, Gaetano, Antonina, and Gaetano

Spouse: Nicolo Cuccia, Piana degli Albanesi, Sicily

Wedding: November 11, 1908, Piana degli Albanesi, Sicily

Children: Jennie, 1911; Paul, 1913; Sam, 1915; and Ann, 1921

Maria Fiorenza Cuccia
August 24, 1885 – 1921

Maria and Nicolo arrived in New York aboard the SS Perguia on January 9, 1910. After living in Boise City, Oklahoma for a few years, they moved to Madison and settled in the Regent and Murray Street neighborhood. The P. Lorillard Tobacco Company was located a long block from the triangle. Maria, like many other Italian immigrants in the neighborhood, found employment there. She died in October, 1921, at age 36.

"Although she died years before I was born, I knew her well from everything my family shared with me. She was a happy person, always singing as she cooked, or dancing around the kitchen with her son, Paul. Although she stood a mere 4-feet, 8-inches, she was a giant of a person. Family was the most important thing in her life. People were so thankful then to be living in America that despite what little they had, they made due and were happy. She sewed clothing from flour sacks for her hourglass figure. She and my grandfather lived at 114 S. Lake Street. After he died, she moved to a second floor apartment over Corona's Market. The family still talks about her lasagna, homemade noodles, and diamond shaped cookies decorated with almonds."

Barbara Cuccia Chase, granddaughter

Nina's Pasta

"This was prepared for me when my grandmother's great-niece, Nina Schiro, visited Madison in 1992.

1/2 onion
Olive oil
1/4 stick of butter
Imported Italian unsalted prosciutto, diced
16-ounce bag of frozen peas
Salt and pepper
1 box of Tripolini or Farfalini (bowtie shaped pastas)
7 3/4-ounces mozzarella cheese (See Note)
1/2 pint heavy whipping cream, unwhipped

Sauté onion in olive oil and butter. Add diced prosciutto, then peas. Season with salt and pepper. Cook pasta; drain. Add to pea/prosciutto mixture. Add cheese, cut into small pieces. Add whipping cream, unwhipped, and serve.

Note: Use mozzarella sold in round balls.

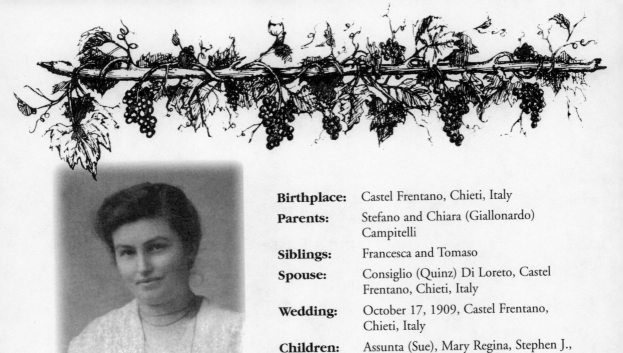

Birthplace:	Castel Frentano, Chieti, Italy
Parents:	Stefano and Chiara (Giallonardo) Campitelli
Siblings:	Francesca and Tomaso
Spouse:	Consiglio (Quinz) Di Loreto, Castel Frentano, Chieti, Italy
Wedding:	October 17, 1909, Castel Frentano, Chieti, Italy
Children:	Assunta (Sue), Mary Regina, Stephen J., Daniel, and Clara

Antonina Campitelli Di Loreto
March 17, 1892 – April 25, 1973

Antonina departed from Italy on the SS American, arriving in New York on February 4, 1914. Several days later she joined her husband in Madison where they settled at 706 Seymour St., remaining there for 45 years. Daughter, Clara, remembers their favorite meal, "polenta on the board." Her mother would pour the polenta onto the large wooden board she used when making homemade noodles. Sections were cut from the polenta to make a map of the United States. A narrow strip was removed to show the Mississippi River and how it flowed when homemade tomato sauce was poured to take the place of the river's water. If there was any polenta left, it was fried the next morning in a skillet with a small amount of oil and served for breakfast.

"She always wore a scarf when she cooked, and a large apron to help keep her hands clean. When she canned, it took many days of standing in the basement to finish all of the bushels of tomatoes, cucumbers, peaches and pears. The stove worked overtime. So did she. When she was done, dozens and dozens of jars filled shelves for the cold months ahead. She sang Italian songs as she worked. When our mother died at age 40, Grandma helped Dad with the five of us kids. It was in the 1960s and the decade became a turbulent time in our lives. With Grandma's help, the bumpy ride got much smoother."

Loretta Tortorice Thompson and Dan Tortorice, grandchildren
(children of Mary Regina)

Polenta

"If there was any polenta left, it was fried the next morning in a skillet with a small amount of oil and served for breakfast."

2 cups coarse grained cornmeal
1 tablespoon salt

Bring 6 1/2 cups of water to a boil in a large heavy kettle. Add salt, turn the heat down to medium low so the water simmers. Add cornmeal in a very thin stream, stirring with a stout, long wooden spoon. Never stop stirring and keep the water at a slow, steady simmer. Stir for 20 minutes or so after all the cornmeal has been added. Polenta is done when it tears away from the sides of the pan as you stir.

Tomato Sauce:
    2 pounds of fresh ripe tomatoes
    1/4 cup olive oil
    1 bunch fresh basil
    1 medium onion, peeled and halved
    1 1/2 teaspoons salt
    1/2 teaspoon granulated sugar

Wash tomatoes in cold water. Cut each in half, lengthwise. Cook in covered saucepan until they have simmered for 10 minutes. Puree tomatoes through a food mill back into the pan. Add oil, basil, onion, salt and sugar and cook at a slow, but steady simmer, uncovered, for 45 minutes. Discard the onion and serve.

Birthplace: San Cipirello, Sicily

Parents: Francisco and Locretzia Alfano

Siblings: Angelina is the youngest of eight children

Spouse: Andrea Di Piazza, Giardinello, Sicily

Wedding: March 13, 1913, San Cipirello, Sicily

Children: Teresa, Laura, Joseph, Frank, Anna, Ann, Salvatore, and Thomas

Angelina Alfano Di Piazza
April 23, 1896 –

*I*n May of 1913, two months after they were married, Angelina and Andrea sailed to America with dreams of a fruitful life together. While residing in Chicago, their first child was born. Later, they moved to the Clementi house at 817 Regent St. in Madison. Several years later, they made their last move to a large two-story, four-bedroom house at 1855 S. Park St. The wood cook stove in the kitchen served a dual purpose, but for additional heating during the cold winter months, a round potbellied stove was placed in the center of the dining room. The house still stands and is described as looking much the same as it did back then. Each spring, Andrea planted a large garden on the corner lot. Tomatoes were in abundance and tomato paste was dried in the sun, shaped in a ball, placed in a crock in the cellar, and covered with olive oil and cheesecloth. Root beer was bottled and stored in the fruit cellar. Andrea's Aunt Vincenza and Uncle Anthony Trapino, who had arrived from Sicily shortly before Angelina and Andrea, and the Trapino's married children with families, all became neighbors.

"It took all Monday to wash clothes. The machine and two tubs for rinsing were in the middle of the kitchen. While my mother worked, she sang to the top of her voice. It was beautiful. Some songs were sad, others romantic. Every two or three days she made bread, always leaving some dough to fry and dunk in sugar and cinnamon. Other times she'd split the fried dough to stuff with jelly or bologna to eat as a sandwich. Everyone had their own place at our big round kitchen table. When friends and relatives came over on weekend evenings, we'd play Italian music on the Victrola. Angelo DeLorenzo played the mandolin and he and my mother would sing ' stornelli.' Joseph Ales would join in. Many years later, after the children had grown, she folded linens on the baby floor at Madison General and St. Mary's Hospital. Until she reached her 95th birthday, she continued to translate letters from Sicily for friends who couldn't read or write the language. She crocheted until she reached her 98th birthday."

Ann Di Piazza Ales, daughter

Sicilian-style Chicken

"We just celebrated her 100th birthday. She was radiant in pink silk and so happy to see friends from the old neighborhood."

**Grated bread crumbs seasoned with
grated Parmesan or Romano cheese,
parsley, salt and pepper (See Note)**
Chicken, cut-up
Egg, beaten
Olive oil
Crushed tomatoes
Potatoes, optional
Peas, optional

Dip chicken in egg wash, then seasoned bread crumbs to coat. Fry until golden brown. Place chicken in roaster, adding some water to prevent it from drying. This will make delicious juice. Place crushed tomatoes over top of chicken pieces. Add peeled potatoes, if desired. Drained peas can be added when chicken is almost done to prevent them from becoming dry. Bake at 350–375 degrees for about 1 1/2 hours or until chicken is done.

Note: Store purchased Italian seasoned bread crumbs can be substituted.

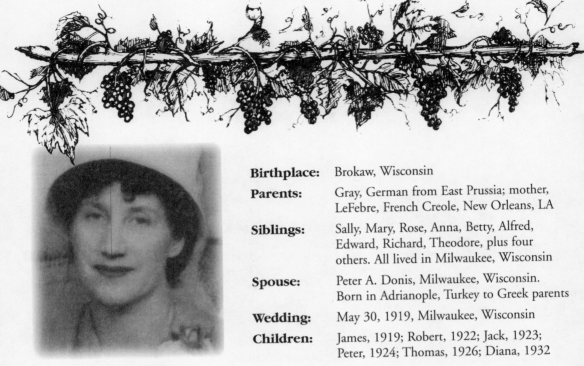

Birthplace:	Brokaw, Wisconsin
Parents:	Gray, German from East Prussia; mother, LeFebre, French Creole, New Orleans, LA
Siblings:	Sally, Mary, Rose, Anna, Betty, Alfred, Edward, Richard, Theodore, plus four others. All lived in Milwaukee, Wisconsin
Spouse:	Peter A. Donis, Milwaukee, Wisconsin. Born in Adrianople, Turkey to Greek parents
Wedding:	May 30, 1919, Milwaukee, Wisconsin
Children:	James, 1919; Robert, 1922; Jack, 1923; Peter, 1924; Thomas, 1926; Diana, 1932

Katherine Gray Donis
September, 1900 – March, 1970

Katherine and Peter Donis moved to Madison on January 1, 1923 and settled at 113 S. Park St. They would remain there until 1940 when the family moved to West Mifflin St. Their Park Street home was a small white bungalow with a spacious yard and white picket fence. Both garden and yard were a source of pride for the family. Each summer Katherine competed with Louisa Audini for honors at the annual flower show held at the Neighborhood House on West Washington Avenue. During the cold months, when the garden was dormant, a potbellied stove provided cozy warmth inside the bungalow. When the heat of summer made days unbearable, the family gathered in a shed attached to the rear of the house that had been converted to a "family room."

"Each day began with my mother starting a fire in the potbellied stove before waking my father for work at the Milwaukee Railroad roundhouse. Like most of the other women in the neighborhood, my mother administered most of the discipline in the family, usually with kindling from the woodpile. As a cook, she mastered lemon, custard, and pumpkin pies, and doughnuts that I especially liked. Although she was raised Roman Catholic, and my father was Greek Orthodox, together they attended the Italian Methodist Church. Rev. Antonio Parroni was quite a salesman. For relaxation, my folks listened to the radio in the evening. It became a nightly ritual. On Saturday night, they went to the tavern next to the Neighborhood House and had a few beers with Italian neighbors. Mrs. DiPiazza from Mound Street, as well as others, taught my mother the secrets to prepare great Italian meals. After she died, a card was found in her handwriting of an Italian relish she made each summer when vegetables had ripened."

Thomas Donis, son

Caponatina

"Although she made excellent pies, some of the Italian women taught her to prepare food Italian-style. This was our favorite."

1 large and 1 small colander of eggplant,
cut in small diamonds (about 10 medium eggplant)
1 small colander of green peppers,
cut fine (about 15 peppers)
1/4 fourth colander of onions, cut fine
1-2 pounds of olives, cut in thirds or fourths,
mashing to squeeze out pits
Fry all in olive oil.

Take two dish pans of tomatoes, cut up and cook, straining and putting in large kettle. Add 1/3 colander of celery, cut in slices. Cook until celery is done. Then, add to this the first mixture which has been fried and browned. Add 2/3 cup cider vinegar, 1 1/2 cups granulated sugar, 3 tablespoons salt, and 1 teaspoon black pepper. Add all together and cook until thick. Can in sterilized jars.

Note: Additional ingredients are listed in the assembling process. The recipe is featured as it appeared on the index card.

Birthplace:	Minsk, Russia
Parents:	Shalom and Bella Sweet
Siblings:	Harry, Mollie, Rose, Arthur, Minnie, and Mae (two brothers died in Russia)
Spouse:	Nathan Dutch, Odessa, Russia
Wedding:	1917
Children:	Sylvia, 1918; Sherman, 1923; and Norris, 1925

Rachel Sweet Dutch
June 8, 1898 –

*S*even years after her father's tragic death in 1907, during which time the Czar was killed, Rachel left her tiny village of straw-thatched roofs. The family would be reunited in Madison. She remembers Madison as a "little place with no sidewalks and hardly any streets." Nathan Dutch, who resided in Chicago, would describe his bride-to-be as a "country girl." Their addresses in the "Bush" would include 207 S. Park St., 41 N. Mills St., and the Robinson House in the 900 block where Milton Street meets Mound St. When Nathan died many years later, Rachel returned to work within walking distance from home at Madison General Hospital. She remembers her independence as well as the strength she needed to carry 100 pound sacks of flour on her shoulder from Sinagub's market on Mound Street. She is a proud woman who enjoys reminiscing to share her experiences with others.

"I remember getting off the train at the Chicago and North-Western Depot. It was frightening not to understand the language here, yet I found work at the Lorillard Tobacco Factory where I stripped leaves as fast as I could to fill each bushel. The work was hard and I got sores on my hands, so I decided to make a change and found a job at the shoe factory on the eastside of town. I had to take a streetcar to get there. But life was good to us here. I enjoyed taking in roomers to help make ends meet. Sherman sold papers for the Wisconsin State Journal at the corner of State St., near the Orpheum Theatre, and Sylvia worked closeby at Blum's. Picnics at Silver Spring, Tenney, and Brittingham parks were very special. If we needed transportation, we'd take a bus and carry a basket filled with spinach borscht, fried breaded veal chops, and homemade bread. Always homemade bread."

Rachel Sweet Dutch

Challah

"I learned to bake this wonderful bread from my mother."

5 pounds of flour
1 stick fresh yeast
1 cup water
2 tablespoons sugar
5 beaten eggs
1 1/2 cups oil
1 cup sugar
1 tablespoon salt

Make a nest in the flour. Combine yeast, water and the small amount of sugar and pour into the nest. Let stand for about 15 minutes. In another bowl, beat 5 eggs. Put a bit of the egg mixture aside. Add 1 1/2 cups oil, 1 cup sugar, and 1 tablespoon of salt to the large egg mixture. Slowly blend egg mixture into flour. Stir, then knead dough for 5 to 10 minutes on a floured board. Place the dough in a well-oiled bowl and let rise in a warm place for about 1 hour. Punch dough down and allow it to rise again.

Divide dough into three parts, and if you plan to braid it, divide each section again into three parts. Braid dough strips and bring ends around to meet. Seal together for a round challah. Oil three 8-inch baking pans, sprinkle with cornmeal, place dough in pans, and cover with a towel. Allow dough to rise in a warm place another 20 to 30 minutes, brush with remaining egg and bake in 350 degree oven for 45 minutes to 1 hour.

Birthplace:	Palermo, Sicily
Parents:	Balthasar and Mariannina Caruso
Siblings:	Carlo and John
Spouse:	Antonio Giuseppe Fiore, Palermo, Sicily
Wedding:	Palermo, Sicily
Children:	Giovanina (Jennie), Anthony J. (A.J.), Salvatore (Sam), Peter, Mary, Louis D., Nicholas John, Frances

Francesca Caruso Fiore
1878 – February 13, 1953

*L*eaving her parents behind, Francesca departed from Palermo for America and Madison with Antonio where they would reside on the first floor of a two-story duplex at 742 Gwinette Court. Francesca, a tiny woman just a bit over five feet tall, wore her dark hair parted in the middle and pinned in a bun at the nape of her neck. Her dresses were ankle-length, however, as she grew older, the hemline rose to mid-calf. Family members cannot recall seeing her without earrings.

"I remember the old-fashioned apron with two big pockets where, in one, a clean handkerchief was tucked, and in the other, hard candies were stored. Like most of the mothers back then, she loved to cook, yet never owned a cookbook. She also took great pride in the garden which ran along the side of the house. If there was a birthday in the family, or any other celebration, she and Grandpa had everyone gather at their place. Other special occasions included the Italian picnics held at Brittingham Park."

Dorothy Triggs, granddaughter

Salsa Fresca Di Pomidoro a la Puttancesca

"Although Grandma recorded not a single recipe, this has been adapted from what is remembered..." Fr. Charles Fiore

> 2 tablespoons olive oil
> 2 to 3 large cloves garlic, chopped or mashed
> 2 small cans flat anchovy filets, drained
>   (or 2 cans rolled anchovy filets with capers)
> 2 pounds fresh Italian plum (Roma-type) tomatoes
> 6 sun-dried tomatoes, chopped
> 2 tablespoons chopped fresh basil (use less if dried)
> 2 tablespoons chopped fresh parsley
> Fresh ground pepper to taste (no salt)

Put olive oil and drained anchovies into large non-stick or stainless steel skillet. Cook anchovies over medium heat, stirring until they begin to dissolve. Add chopped/mashed garlic. Sauté an additional 3 minutes.

Blanch tomatoes quickly in boiling water, and peel (may leave skins on if you prefer). Chop into small pieces and add to oil, anchovy, garlic mixture. Cook until tomatoes also begin to dissolve. Add remaining ingredients of sun-dried tomatoes, basil and parsley. Simmer uncovered over low heat until sauce thickens. Adjust seasonings with garlic and pepper. Mix small amount of sauce with cooked pasta. Reserve and pour remainder over individual servings. Sufficient for 2 people and 1 pound of pasta.

Note: Tomato pieces make this a chunky sauce. Since anchovies are salty, no additional salt is needed. Cooking does away with their fishy taste and leaves only a piquant flavor. I've fed this sauce to anchovy-haters, who loved it. Try it first without cheese as I believe cheese masks its distinctive flavor.

Birthplace:	Minsk, Russia
Parents:	not available
Siblings:	Jacob
Spouse:	William Frank, Minsk, Russia
Wedding:	not available
Children:	Minnie, 1921; Frances, 1925; Alfred Aaron, 1931

Rose Leiberman Frank
1899 – 1968

Rose Leiberman arrived in this country in 1913 with her brother, Jacob, who previously had settled in Chicago. In 1921, she and her husband, William Frank, established themselves in Madison in the Greenbush neighborhood where she operated a grocery store at 118 S. Park Street, next to Schwartz's Drug Store. The Leiberman's lived at the same address until the 1960s when urban renewal changed the structure and ingredients of the old neighborhood.

"My mother was totally committed to the family. We lived behind the grocery store and she would wake up early to put coal in the furnace. She did the usual cooking for us—baked, washed clothes, cleaned the house—and in between, tended to customers. The name of the store was 'Bill's Food Store.' My father wasn't quite as tactful with customers as my mother was, so she more or less handled that end of it. About the only relaxation she had took place during evening hours when she'd sew clothes for us kids while listening to the radio. She had such a thirst for knowledge and read the Jewish newspaper, The Daily Forward, from cover to cover. Because it was important to blend in with American culture, she attended evening classes at the Neighborhood House at 768 West Washington Avenue and learned to spell and read the English language."

Frances Mann, daughter

Wine Cake

*"She was the biggest flag waver of all in her newly adopted country.
She loved it here."*

12 eggs, separated
1 cup sugar
1 cup wine
1 cup matzo cake meal
1/2 teaspoon salt
1 teaspoon cinnamon
1 cup ground walnuts

Cream egg yolks with sugar, beating until very light. Add wine, cake meal, salt, cinnamon, and nuts. Fold in stiffly beaten egg whites. Bake in a tube pan with a removable bottom at 325 degrees for approximately one hour. Invert pan and allow cake to cool before removing.

Birthplace:	Piana degli Albanesi, Sicily
Parents:	Giovanbattista and Concetta (Russoto) Musso
Siblings:	not available
Spouse:	Vincent Gallina, Piana degli Albanesi, Sicily
Wedding:	July 7, 1921
Children:	Tina (Connie), 1922; Josephine, 1924; Sam, 1932

Vincenzia Musso Gallina
February 20, 1897 – August 17, 1987

*A*rriving in America was not as joyous an event as Vincenza and Vincent had planned. Accompanying them on the voyage was Vincenza's father, Giovanbattista, who became ill during the trip. When their vessel docked in Boston, Massachusetts that day in October of 1921, authorities immediately quarantined him for the required time, forcing the newly married couple to lodge at a nearby hotel until they all could travel to Madison where many others from their village awaited their arrival. Housing in Madison was established in the second house from the busy corner of Park and Regent streets. Vincenza's kitchen at 821 S. Park Street was large, bright, cheerful, and aromatic. Although spaghetti was a family favorite, there was an abundance of homemade Italian sausage, homemade noodles and breaded round steak as a fragrant reminder of their native cooking. Friends and family often gathered in the kitchen, especially during the holidays to make cookies.

"Days were busy for our mother, but restful times came after evening meals when she would walk down to Zia Josephine's (Corona) where the two would sit and chat in front of the grocery store. It seemed soothing for them to reminisce. She also loved sitting with her best friend, Maria Gervasi. If they wanted to have cake with coffee, they'd bake one. It never mattered what time of night it was. Another fond recollection is of the wedding celebrations and other parties held at the Italian Workmen's Club on Regent Street. Pool tables were pushed to one side of the room, then covered with blankets to make beds for all the little ones while the parents sang and danced."

Sam Gallina, Tina Gwinn, and Jo Palermo

Tannilucci

"This delicate biscotti was a favorite of Mama's..."

6 eggs, well beaten
1 shot glass of brandy
Juice and grated rind of one orange
3 cubes of butter (1 1/2 cups of butter)
2 1/3 cups sugar
10 cups all-purpose flour
4 tablespoons baking powder

Beat eggs and add brandy, juice and grated rind; set aside. Cream butter and sugar; add egg mixture and mix well. Mix flour and baking powder and place in large bowl. Make a well and add eggs and butter mixture to the flour; proceed to mix and knead. Let dough rest. An extra cup of flour may be used if dough is sticky. Continue to knead. Roll dough into 1/8-inch thick strips about 2-inches long and 1-inch wide to form little crowns. Bake on a cookie sheet at 350 degrees for about 15 minutes. Watch closely as they should be lightly brown in color. Cool on a rack for 30 minutes. Ice with glaze of powdered sugar and juice of an orange thin enough to use with a pastry brush. Sprinkle with nonpareils. Makes dozens of cookies. When forming crowns, you may need to trim as you go to form the crowns.

Note: Crisco can be substituted for half the butter, if desired.

Birthplace:	Passo di Rigano, Sicily
Parents:	Franco and Theresa (Marinno) Caruso
Siblings:	Stephano, Giovanno, Baptista, Rose, Madaglina, Salvatore, and Vincenza
Spouse:	Peter Gambino, Palermo, Sicily
Wedding:	March 14, 1920, Sicily
Children:	Steve, Frank, Theresa, Mary, Ann, Peter, Jr.

Madaglina Caruso Gambino
August 15, 1897 – February 13, 1978

*P*eter Gambino was only 17 years old when he arrived in Madison to live with his sister, Josephine, and her husband, Alphonse Chiovaro. It was during a period of unrest, however, and a decision was necessary to either stay in the United States and fight for his new country, or return to Sicily. Although he decided to stay, he returned to Sicily to see his family before being sent to France. While in Sicily, he passed by Madaglina Caruso who was washing clothes outdoors with her friends, Rose Guastella, Rose DiCristina, and Rose Prestigiacomo. Gambino sensed Madaglina would someday become his wife. When the war ended, the two were married. When they came to America, they stayed with the Chiovaros and another sister, Rose, and her husband, Anton Urso. Later, Madaglina and Peter would purchase a house at 129 S. Murray St.

"My mother lived for her family. Cooking, cleaning, canning, baking lots of bread, and many different kinds of spaghetti. We ate lots of spaghetti. When we'd get home from school at St. Joseph's, we could smell sauce cooking and bread baking. She used to give us a small bowl of sauce and bread to hold us over until the evening meal was served at 6 o'clock when my father returned home from work at the railroad roundhouse. Wonderful times were spent getting together with her cousin, Rosalia and Tony Caruso, or with Ursos or Chiovaros. Sunday afternoons meant having dinner with Joe and Rose Guastella. My mother was very religious, going to church all the time and lighting candles. She prayed so hard. Every Tuesday night was Novena night at St. James. When my brother Frank was killed at Iwo Jima on March 3, 1945, her world fell apart. And then, in 1960, when she learned they had to move from the "Bush," it was another heartache and loss. My father missed his big garden and the large screen porch where they sat after supper, either alone or with relatives. All of that changed. The good times ended for everyone."

Theresa Gambino Pfeiffer, daughter

Panelli

"We used to have this often. The flour was purchased at Caruso's White Front Grocery store on the corner of Lake and Mound streets, but today it's available at the Mifflin Community Co-op on N. Bassett St."

1 pound chickpea flour
1 1/2 quarts water
2 teaspoons salt
1 teaspoon pepper
1/2 cup chopped fresh parsley

Bring water to boil; add flour, stirring to prevent lumping. Stir until thick; add parsley. When it is thick enough to spread, have a lightly oiled board ready to spread dough about 1/2-inch thick, or thinner. Let dry and cut into squares. Turn on opposite side and dry again. Fry in hot oil until light brown. Put on a warm bun or buttered bread. This makes a good sandwich.

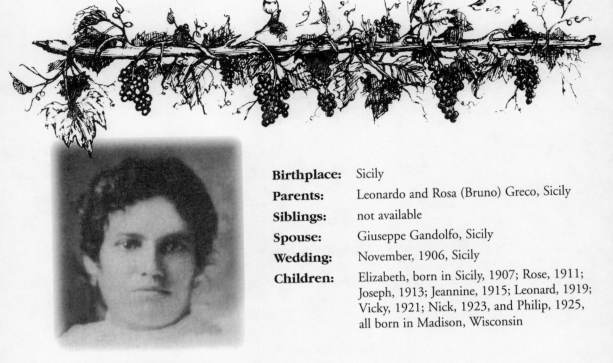

Birthplace:	Sicily
Parents:	Leonardo and Rosa (Bruno) Greco, Sicily
Siblings:	not available
Spouse:	Giuseppe Gandolfo, Sicily
Wedding:	November, 1906, Sicily
Children:	Elizabeth, born in Sicily, 1907; Rose, 1911; Joseph, 1913; Jeannine, 1915; Leonard, 1919; Vicky, 1921; Nick, 1923, and Philip, 1925, all born in Madison, Wisconsin

Giacoma Greco Gandolfo
February 21, 1887 – September 18, 1926

The Gandolfo children were raised at 816 Regent Street in one of the few houses that remain from the old neighborhood. As a rooming house on Hamilton Street near the Capitol Square, it had been scheduled for demolition. Having been purchased, it was moved over unpaved roads of dirt and mud to the Greenbush plat where it was converted to a two-family residence. Gandolfos lived in a sparsely furnished apartment on the second floor, heated during the winter months with coal carried by Giacoma in buckets from the basement. She was a meticulous person who kept her stove immaculate at all times. Her pride and joy, however, was the Singer Sewing machine used to make clothes for the family. Each week 15 loaves of bread were baked in a stone oven in the basement, then removed with a long handled metal paddle made by Guiseppe. Clothes were washed each day in a large metal tub with a wooden washboard also made by her husband. Described as a tiny woman with brown eyes and dark curly hair, she barely reached five feet tall. Giacoma Gandolfo died at age 39.

"I cannot remember her ever losing her temper with any of us. Although she missed her parents and sisters back in Sicily, she never complained. Most of the food she prepared was Sicilian. The large kitchen had a pantry and enough chairs for us to sit together around the table. The sink was in the hallway. When she made bread, she'd break off pieces to flatten, then fry like pancakes. We'd sprinkle them with sugar and devour each one. When Easter arrived, she made baskets and birds from sweetened bread dough and placed hard-boiled eggs in the dough before baking. Christmas meant fig cookies and other ethnic delicacies."

Elizabeth Gandolfo Saffioti, daughter

Eggplant Parmesan

"The oven in the basement had to be fired with wood until it was just the right temperature. When it was ready, we'd help carry loaves of bread to bake from the second floor kitchen."

**2 eggplant, total of 3 pounds, peeled and sliced
    about 1/2-inch thick
2 eggs, beaten with 2 tablespoons of milk
Bread crumbs, flavored with cheese, garlic powder
    and parsley flakes (seasoned crumbs)
2 quarts of homemade spaghetti sauce
1 pound chunk mozzarella cheese**

Put eggplant slices in colander, salting each layer. Let drain about 1 to 2 hours. Rinse off with cold water to remove salt. Lay slices on a clean dish towel and pat dry. Dip in egg mixture, then crumbs, shaking off excess crumbs lightly. Place on well-buttered cookie sheets. Drizzle small amount of olive oil over top. Bake in 350 degrees oven. When lightly brown on one side, turn to allow other side to brown. Test doneness with fork. Cool. These can be made the day before. Layer in a deep 8 by 8-inch pan beginning with sauce, then eggplant, mozzarella; repeat, ending with mozzarella. If you have another pan the same size, cover pan, bottom side up, to allow room for cheese to cook without sticking. Otherwise, cover loosely with aluminum foil. Bake in a 350 degree oven until hot throughout, removing cover near the end.

Note: Choose slim eggplant to avoid abundance of seeds. Do not prepare dish when browned eggplant slices are hot as mozzarella will melt and become gooey.

Birthplace:	Piana degli Albanesi, Sicily
Parents:	Anthony and Lucia (DiGiorgio) Magro
Siblings:	Joseph, Vito, and Georgia
Spouse:	Vito Gervasi, Piana degli Albanesi, Sicily
Wedding:	February 5, 1911
Children:	Mary, 1911; Lucy, 1913; Joe, 1914; Tony, 1916; John, 1918; Sam, 1920; Ann, 1922

Maria Magro Gervasi
February 24, 1891 – August 20, 1990

The Magro family emigrated to this country in 1906 and settled in Chicago, Illinois. In 1914, Maria and her husband, Vito Gervasi, moved to 1 South Murray Street in Madison in a three-story apartment building where a market and butcher shop was arranged on the first floor. The building had two apartments on second floor and two apartments on third floor, one of which would serve as bedrooms for the Gervasi family. Maria tended the store, cut meat, cared for her family, and studied at Neighborhood House to become an American citizen. When friends and family from their village in Sicily arrived in Madison, they would stay in the rooms upstairs until permanent lodging was established. Although Maria relaxed by knitting and crocheting beautiful items to give to others, she also loved to play Scopa. Her talents as a story teller stimulated the imaginations of young and old during precious hours shared around the potbellied stove.

"I remember Mom and her neighbors, Josephine Corona, Maria Pellitteri, Sasida Provenzano, and Felicia Pullara gathering in the afternoon to knit, crochet, mend and tell stories. Sometimes, when the stories were a little on the "shady" side, they would burst out laughing in embarrassment. Late in the summer, when the tomatoes ripened, they'd put their needles and crochet hooks aside to stir and cook tomatoes to spread on large boards to dry. After the tomatoes had thickened in the hot sun, the paste was shaped with their hands and placed in crocks. When each ball of paste had been covered with a layer of olive oil, the crocks were stored in the basement. A small amount of this was used throughout the year when spaghetti sauce was made."

Lucy Corona and Ann Schiro, daughters

Sfinge

"She just loved playing tricks on us when we were little kids. Sometimes she'd wrap dough around a cotton ball before deep frying the dough. She always made at least four or five sfinge like this. It was always fun to see who got the sfinge with cotton inside."

3 eggs, room temperature
2 cups milk
2 tablespoons sugar
2 teaspoons vanilla
1 tablespoon baking powder
3 cups flour
3 cups vegetable oil to deep fry

Beat together eggs, milk, and sugar. Add vanilla. Mix together flour and baking powder, then combine with egg mixture. Drop pieces of dough in hot oil and deep fry until golden brown. Remove, place on paper toweling, then shake gently in paper bag containing sugar, or sugar and cinnamon. Serve warm.

Note: Recipe can be easily doubled.

Birthplace:	Middleton, Wisconsin
Parents:	Irish/English parents arrived in Wisconsin from Carlingford, Ireland, in July, 1863.
Siblings:	not available
Spouse:	Leroy Gyles, of Irish and English ancestry
Wedding:	1910
Children:	Minnie, James, and Maude

Ida Robbins Gyles
August 31, 1889 – June 27, 1979

Ida and Leroy's first dwelling in the Greenbush neighborhood was a small, third floor apartment at 720 Mound Street with Loniello's occupying first floor, and Onheibers as next door neighbors. Later, the Gyles purchased a small white two-story house at 24 S. Murray St. During the cold winter months, Ida rose early to warm the kitchen with wood and coal. There were times, however, when the cold running water in the small sink froze. Weekly baths were taken in a wash basin placed in front of a wood stove that rested on a linoleum covered floor. Despite description, the home was her castle. When she passed away, the farthest she had traveled in her 90 years was to visit northern Illinois.

"I knew Grandma as "Boogie" When she was 50, she cared for me and my brother so my mother could work. Later, "Boogie" took on another job to support us. Every day she got up at 4 a.m. to sort through papers and rags at Sinaiko's to make tidy bundles to sell. From there she would head out to Shorewood, which she referred to as 'Big Bug Hill,' to clean houses. Although she was a tiny person, she loved to tell about the day she saw a neighborhood bully teasing a young girl. When she saw a grass snake slither by, she grabbed the snake and put it inside the back of the boy's pants. Every time she told the story, she would slap her knee and laugh. When the Triangle Project offered a pittance for her home, her years suddenly became evident. Maybe the house was simple, the linoleum worn, and the screen door a bit rusty, but it was hers and it was spotless, and she was so proud of it. I think that was the first time grandma died a little."

Heather, great-granddaughter
(daughter of Phyllis Gyles Lingard)

Navy Bean Soup

"I knew Grandma as 'Boogie.'"

1 package navy beans
1 medium onion
1 bay leaf
2 carrots, sliced
Salt and pepper
1 ham bone (preferably) or 1/4 pound ham, diced

Soak beans in large bowl overnight with a teaspoon of baking soda in the water (this prevents the formation of gas in the stomach). Next morning, drain off water and put in a large pan. Cover beans with fresh water, diced onion, bay leaf, diced carrots, ham bone or diced ham, salt and pepper. Cook slowly for 4 or 5 hours, or until beans are soft. Serve with French bread.

Birthplace: Palermo (Monreale), Sicily

Parents: Lorenzo and Pietra (Intravaia) Intravaia

Siblings: Philip

Spouse: Calogero Intravaia, Palermo, Sicily

Wedding: August 9, 1909, Monreale, Sicily

Children: Vito, 1909; Conchera (Connie) 1911; Pietrina (Beatrice) 1912; Saridda (Sara) 1914; Maria (Marie) 1913; Tomessina, 1917; Antonina (Anne) 1918; Lorenzo (Larry) 1919; Tomasso (Thomas) 1921; Sam, 1922; Philip, 1924; Sally, and Rita

Margherita Intravaia Intravaia
August 26, 1887 – April 20, 1957

March 1912 would mark their arrival in Madison. There was much activity in the two-story house at 819 Milton St. where Margherita served as a mediator to calm matters that arose during the course of any day. Mealtimes were massive celebrations with enough food prepared "just in case" someone, or two or more, stopped by to visit. The Intravaia kitchen, large by today's standards, was the gathering room for the family. During the early morning hours, coffee with milk, pastries and homemade bread were made plentiful for breakfast. Family celebrations took place in the dining room where men would play cards after dishes were removed. This was a talented household where music often reigned. Italian songs were sung while cleaning, washing, ironing or during any mode of relaxation. As a deeply religious person, Margherita attended Mass often at St. Joseph's Catholic Church, directly across the street from their market and home at 27 S. Park St., where they had moved in 1920.

"I remember seeing her only once. I was four years old, but still recall her standing at the stove and smiling down at me as she stirred a big kettle. I was a little frightened of the language, especially when they talked loudly. My father assured me that no one was angry...it was just the way Italians talked."

Leah Intravaia Younker, granddaughter
(daughter of Tom)

"She had an apron that seemed to have magical bottomless pockets. It seemed that anytime we asked her for something, she'd pull it from the depths of her pockets...like everything we needed was always there."

Thomas Intravaia, son

Almond Slices with Cherries

"She was an excellent cook, making both Italian and American dishes. I still remember the way the house smelled..."
Michael Marinaro, grandson (son of Sarah)

8 eggs
2 cups sugar
1 teaspoon vanilla and 1 tiny drop of anise oil
1 tablespoon milk
6 cups flour
2 level teaspoons baking powder
1/2 pound butter, melted
Almonds, toasted and chopped
1 4-ounce jar of maraschino cherries,
        drained and chopped

Beat eggs and add sugar, vanilla and milk. Mix well. Sift dry ingredients and add melted butter. Mix all ingredients together with nuts and cherries. Chill dough in refrigerator until it is ready to handle. Roll out into long loaves, as in making biscotti, and pat about 1/2-inch thick. Bake at 350 degrees until golden brown on bottom and just slightly set on top. Do not overbake. When loaves are cool, frost and slice.

Note: *Cookies are even prettier using red and green cherries.* Anne Intravaia Cerniglia

Birthplace: San Giuseppe, Sicily

Parents: Reda

Siblings: Joseph

Spouse: Frank LaBarro

Wedding: 1904, San Giuseppe, Sicily

Children: Rosina, 1905; Sam, 1907; Peter, 1909; John, 1911; Angelo, 1913

Serifina Reda LaBarro
1878 – 1972

Serifina and Frank LaBarro arrived in this country with their baby, Rosina, in 1906 and settled in a two-story wooden house on Desmond Court in Madison that had been built sometime during the late 1800s. While her husband worked as a laborer on the construction of the State Capitol from 1914-1918, Serifina tended their children and stripped leaves at the Lorillard Tobacco warehouse, behind Dominic Audini's house on Proudfit St., near Lake Monona.

"She was a great cook. I remember hearing that she had to lock the cabinets in the kitchen to keep my dad and his brothers from eating all the homemade bread stored inside."

Angelo LaBarro, grandson
(son of Angelo)

"I was only sixteen when Angelo first took me to their truck farm. On the way, he told me to remember, no matter what, that his mother was always right. That sheds a little light on the respect he had for her. There was no problem honoring his request. She was so very good to me. Other than a language barrier, I couldn't have asked for a nicer mother-in-law. She was a hard worker. During the winter months, she stripped leaves at the Lorillard Tobacco Company. When spring arrived, her place was at the farm. It was located where the Dane County Coliseum is today. Although she was about 5 feet tall, and just as wide, she worked from sun up to sun down in the garden. If she wasn't picking berries, she was getting produce ready to sell. Sundays were days of rest. Friends and family would drive up from Rockford, for spaghetti-on-the-boards outdoors. On Thanksgiving, I helped by preparing the turkey with rice stuffing. When it was done, we'd put the pan in the trunk of the car and head to the farm. She'd have the oven warm and waiting."

Pauline LaBarro, daughter-in-law
(wife of Angelo)

Sicilian Ricotta Puffs, LaBarro Style

"This was a common recipe in the neighborhood...a Sicilian 'quick lunch'..."

Make batch of yeast bread dough. Shape little round loaves of bread about 4 inches in diameter and 1-inch thick and place on pan. Set on a clean sheet spread on the bed. Cover with another sheet. Allow dough to rise to 3 1/4-inches high; dust loaves with flour. Place in a preheated 350 degree oven and bake until bread is light brown on top, but not yet fully cooked. Put back on sheet on bed and cover again with an extra sheet as they will continue to rise, becoming soft enough to cut easier.

Stuff bread rolls with fresh ricotta cheese, salt and pepper. The hot buns will partially melt or warm the stuffing, whatever is used. Another version is using olive oil and freshly grated Romano cheese. Either way, the "puffs" are very tasty.

Birthplace:	San Giuseppe Iato, Sicily
Parents:	Salvatore and Francesca Gandolfo
Siblings:	Mary, Paul, Catherine, Providence and Grace
Spouse:	Pietro LaBruzzo
Wedding:	San Giuseppe Iato, Sicily
Children:	Calogero, born in Sicily; Salvatore, born in Brooklyn, N.Y.; Frances, Grace, Joseph, Catherine, Mary, Stella, born in Madison, Wisconsin

Antonina Gandolfo La Bruzzo
December 30, 1891 – September 1978

A traditional preparation of marrying in Sicily was for a man to kidnap the young woman of his choice. It was the method used when Pietro LaBruzzo decided he wanted Antonina Gandolfo, age 16, as his wife. Later, when Pietro and his uncle sailed for America to find work and a place to live, Antonina would remain in Sicily with their first born son. After being reunited in New York, and the birth of another son, LaBruzzos packed up and moved to Madison to a two-story, three-bedroom house at 708 Milton St. where they would celebrate the arrival of seven more children.

"Each day Mother's morning was occupied with cooking in preparation for the large meal our father expected at noon. She was a great cook who made certain we had much more than just spaghetti to eat. Steak was our father's favorite, so she served it often. During the Depression it seemed that she fed half the neighborhood. She loved doing things like that. At Christmastime, she baked extra cookies, sfinge and pignolata to share with others. Anyone who stopped by the house was expected to sit down and eat. We always had company. If we didn't have our friends there, it was Carlo Caputo or Mr. DiSalvo stopping by. She was a very religious person. Hanging over the refrigerator in the kitchen was a picture of God. Other holy pictures in the house were of Jesus, St. Joseph, and the Blessed Mother. What did she do in her spare time after keeping a house immaculate with nine children? She prayed the rosary, attended Mass, or sat on the front porch."

Catherine Alberici and Stella Gargano, daughters

Pignolata

"One of her favorites..."

2 cups of flour
1/4 teaspoon salt
3 eggs
Oil for deep-frying
16-ounces of honey

Mix together first three ingredients to make dough. Cut dough into strips of six inches, then cut into very small pieces. When all dough is used up, fry in hot oil until light in color. Bring honey to boil, then simmer for about ten minutes. Mix all balls into honey, then remove from kettle and mound like a pyramid on a large plate. Sprinkle with cinnamon, then a dusting of powdered sugar. Confetti candy and nonpareils can be used to garnish the pignolata pyramid.

Birthplace:	Piana degli Albanesi, Sicily
Parents:	Guidera
Siblings:	Conchera
Spouse:	John Licali, Piana degli Albanesi, Sicily
Wedding:	Piana degli Albanesi, Sicily
Children:	Dominic, George, Mary, Elizabeth, Ninfa, and Victoria

Josephine Guidera Licali
1860s – 1940

Accompanied by her four daughters, widow Josephine Licali sailed for the United States to settle in New Orleans where her sons, Dominic and George, arrived earlier to work the sugar plantation fields. When George moved north to Wisconsin, the rest of the family followed, except for Dominic who chose to remain in Louisiana. The family settled in a three-flat in Madison at 826 Regent St., next door to the Capadona family at the intersection of Park and Regent streets. As an employee of city and private contractor John Icke, George planned another move, this time to Rockford, Illinois where he became owner of the Rockford Celery Company which supplied fresh produce to local business, and grapes to families to make homemade wine. When Josephine's youngest daughter, Ninfa, married Vito Capadona, she moved in with the newlyweds and remained with them until her death at the onset of World War II.

"Although my grandmother was a hard worker, I can't remember ever seeing her prepare a meal. Our time together was after the meal when dishes were washed. She was an excellent seamstress and made all the skirts and blouses she wore, as well as all the mending, without ever wearing glasses. But most important, she was a midwife and delivered most of the babies in our Regent St. neighborhood."

Conchera Capadona Pullara, daughter

"I can see her as plain as if I looked out the window today. Every morning at 6:30 she'd wrap herself in a shawl, walk down Regent St. and cross to the other side of W. Washington Ave. to strip leaves at the Lorillard tobacco factory. I think she was paid two cents per pound back then. My brother, Joe, worked there, and so did I for a short time when I was 16. She stayed there until sometime prior to World War II when she decided it was time to 'retire'."

John Scalissi, grandson
(son of Elizabeth, also known as "Tukya")

Conchera's Garlic Sauce

*"She was an excellent seamstress, but I can't remember ever
seeing her cook a meal."*

2 garlic cloves, chopped
Olive oil
1 8-ounce can tomato sauce
Salt and pepper to taste
Oregano
Fresh lemon juice

Sauté garlic in olive oil until very light golden in color. Do not brown as garlic will
become bitter. Add tomato sauce and season with salt and pepper. Simmer for 110 minutes.
Add oregano and lemon juice.

Birthplace:	Palermo, Sicily
Parents:	Vitale
Siblings:	Tony
Spouse:	Pietro Magnasco, Palermo, Sicily
Wedding:	1900, Palermo, Sicily
Children:	John, 1902; Rose, 1904; Peter, 1907

Nunzia Vitale Magnasco
1878 – 1948

*L*ife was expected to change for Pietro Magnasco in 1908 after gaining sponsorship from relatives to sail for America in search of a better life for he and his family. After three years of a lonely and frugal existence in Madison, Wisconsin, he sent for his family. When they sailed into the New York harbor, Nunzia and others thought the Statue of Liberty was the Blessed Virgin. Upon completion of the immigrant processing procedures on Ellis Island, a train was boarded for Madison where Pietro had rented a house with plans to convert the small living room into a mini-grocery store. As his business grew, the need for larger quarters became imperative and the Magnasco grocery store was built on the right northeast corner of Milton and Frances streets at 614 Milton Street. Although the building was not constructed until 1912, "established 1910" was printed on the Frances street side of the building.

"My grandfather died at age 35 from a molar infection. It was during the early 1920s and times were very rough. My grandmother continued to operate the store by herself and with the help of her children. I don't remember her for her cooking skills. In fact, the only food I ever saw her cook was pasta. But I do remember how she dried tomatoes on wood boards outside in the hot sun, just like everyone else did in the Milton Street neighborhood. However, my mother recalls how she prepared the fish her little brothers caught in Lake Monona, as well as wild greens and wild mushrooms she, herself, picked in the neighborhood."

Peter Fumusa, grandson
(son of Rose)

Italian Potato Soup

"When they arrived in the New York harbor, Grandma thought the Statue of Liberty was the Virgin Mary..."

1 garlic clove, finely chopped
1 tablespoon olive oil
4 medium red potatoes, peeled and cut in small chunks
2-4 tablespoons chopped parsley
Salt and pepper to taste
3 cups chicken broth
2 eggs, beaten

In a 2-quart saucepan, sauté garlic in oil. Add potatoes, parsley, salt and pepper and chicken broth. Bring to a boil, then simmer about 15 minutes or until potatoes are tender. Add beaten eggs in a steady stream while stirring constantly. When eggs have thickened, serve. Serves 4

Note: To make asparagus soup, substitute 1 bunch asparagus for potatoes and one small chopped onion for garlic.

Birthplace:	Piana degli Albanesi, Sicily
Parents:	not available
Siblings:	Nick, Henry, and Mary
Spouse:	Angelo Maisano
Wedding:	1905, Piana degli Albanesi, Sicily
Children:	Rose; Anna, 1908; Mary, 1910; Joe "Maxie", 1912.

Anna Cuccia Maisano
1879 – 1934

*A*nna and Angelo Maisano were early arrivals in Madison and established their home at 821 Regent Street. In 1927, construction was completed on their new two-story brick building a block away at 912 Regent St. Maisano's grocery store would operate on the first floor, while living quarters for the family occupied second floor. When Anna's husband passed away in 1930, the store was reduced in size to make living arrangements for Anna at the rear of the store.

"When I was young, I preferred a can of Franco-American to my mother's homemade spaghetti. I also remember that my mother couldn't read or write. Although many customers charged grocery items back then, she logged each transaction with a variety of lines and marks. When my sister Anna returned home from school at the end of the day, she would ask who had stopped by and what they had charged. As my mother "read" from her notes, Anna would transfer the information to a sheet of paper for the only record the store would have on file."

Mary Maisano DiSalvo, daughter

"I can't remember my grandmother relaxing. At one time, the store was the only one in the immediate neighborhood. It seemed that the hours were very long and she worked every one of them. Yet, I remember her kindness and how sweet she was. The only time spent outside of the store and apartment was to visit her two brothers and sister. Oftentimes, I would go along with her when she visited Aunt Mary and Uncle Frank (Parisi) a few blocks away on Spring Street. Another recollection is that as a widow, she always wore black. Like Grandpa, she died at a young age."

Vinci DiSalvo, granddaughter
(daughter of Mary)

Nonna Maisano's Fried Potatoes and Eggs

"This was a good Friday meal for the family."

4-5 potatoes, peeled and sliced
4-5 eggs, scrambled
1 large onion, optional, cut into slices
1 large green pepper, optional, cut into slices
Salt and pepper

In large cast iron frying pan, add enough olive oil to cover bottom of pan. Fry potatoes until light brown. Add onions and peppers and cook, covered, for about 10 minutes. Add eggs to ingredients. Salt and pepper to taste. Brown on one side, then divide in half and flip to other side.

Birthplace: Piana degli Albanesi, Sicily

Parents: Saverio and Giovanna Matranga

Grandparents: Teodore and Giovanna (Salamone) Matranga
Great-grandparents: Giuseppe and Francesca (Schiro) Matranga

Siblings: Giovanna, Theodore, and Demetri

Spouse: Giuseppe Maisano, Piana degli Albanesi, Sicily

Wedding: January 13, 1912, Piana degli Albanesi, Sicily

Children: Vito, 1913; Joseph, 1914; Mary, 1916; Jenny, 1919; Samuel, 1923; Richard, 1929

Giuseppa Matranga Maisano
March 7, 1889 – August 8, 1983

Giuseppa Matranga met Giuseppe Maisano one day as he passed by her home on his way to work. Forty-five days following his discharge from the Italian Army, after serving six months in Tripoli, the two were married. Eight months later, Giuseppe left for the United States with his 17-year old brother-in-law Tony Matranga. They joined Giuseppe's brother, Giorgio, who had been living in Madison since 1909. Two months later, back in Sicily, Giuseppa gave birth to a son, Vito, who expired shortly after birth. On October 8, 1913, Giuseppa, her parents and their close friend, Tony Fabiano, departed from Piana degli Albanesi for Madison. When they boarded the SS San Guglielmo in Palermo, each carried a total of $50.00. They arrived in New York City on October 24, 1913. Waiting their arrival in Madison was a house Giuseppe's first cousin, Joe Wrend, built at 14 N. Murray St. They shared the dwelling with the Guistis, and Tony Matranga. In 1919, they moved to 110 S. Lake Street and into a house referred to as "the house on stilts" because of it being surrounded by marshland. On September 16, 1929, at the age of 40, Giuseppa Matranga Maisano became an American citizen.

"I remember her fig cookies at Christmastime. They were very special and she made them in huge quantities. Unlike many other grandmothers during that era, she wrote down some recipes on small pieces of paper. However, because everything was measured in jelly glasses, it is difficult today to determine the exact amount of ingredients she used. And besides, each was written in her native language, none of which I can read. This recipe for Italian sausage and potatoes was one of her favorites, as well as ours. There are no amounts, but it is fairly easy to figure out."

Gina Maisano, granddaughter
(daughter of Joseph)

Italian Sausage and Potatoes

*"Grandma wrote down all her recipes in Albanian–
this is one we figured out on our own."*

Italian sausage links, mild flavor
Potatoes
Salt and pepper to taste
Onion slices
Green pepper
Stewed tomatoes

Brown sausage links and place in the bottom of large roasting pan. Quarter potatoes and lay over sausages. Season with salt and pepper. Lay green pepper and onion slices over potatoes. Place stewed tomatoes over the top. Cover and bake at 375 degrees for about an hour or until potatoes are done.

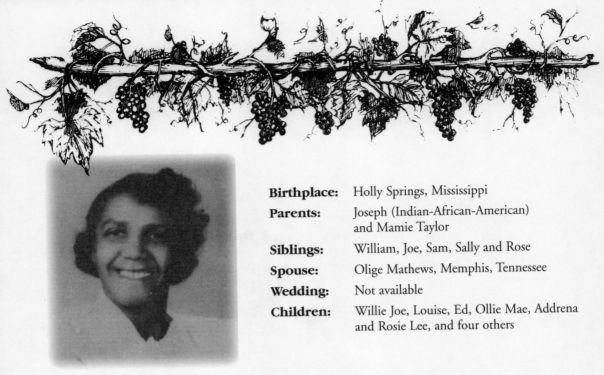

Birthplace:	Holly Springs, Mississippi
Parents:	Joseph (Indian-African-American) and Mamie Taylor
Siblings:	William, Joe, Sam, Sally and Rose
Spouse:	Olige Mathews, Memphis, Tennessee
Wedding:	Not available
Children:	Willie Joe, Louise, Ed, Ollie Mae, Addrena and Rosie Lee, and four others

Mamie Taylor Mathews
July 29, 1883 – December 23, 1979

The Mathews arrived in the Greenbush neighborhood in 1923. Their kitchen at 809 Mound Street was small, yet comfortable. The kitchen was much larger when they moved to 617 Milton Street. Later, when they lived in an apartment over Troia's Market at 754 W. Washington Avenue, the kitchen, as well as the rest of the living quarters, was large, very neat, and very comfortable. Wherever Mamie Mathews prepared food, it was always in abundance, especially when making bread and rolls. Other specialties were cakes, apple pies, sweet potato pies and peach cobblers.

"Because my mother was very active in the Mt. Zion Baptist Church on West Johnson Street, Sunday meant "all-day" religion. At 9:30 a.m., she'd haul us all to church. Since our Sunday food was prepared on Saturday, it all worked out pretty good as we'd stay at church until 1:30 in the afternoon, then return home to eat. At 5:30 we'd be back at church for the entire evening. By 10 p.m., we'd head for home. It was the weekend ritual, never changing, no matter what kind of weather we had."

"Yellow cake was one of her specialties. She liked to serve it warm from the oven, without icing. Like many others in the 'Bush', she learned how to make spaghetti from our Italian neighbors. Falci's lived directly across from us and we all visited back and forth or gathered on each other's porches. She used to can everything, but once she found out what was available in cans at the grocery store, her canning days ended. Although times were often pretty frugal for us, it was watch-out-for-Christmas! That was celebration time. Shopping was done by walking to Hill's Department Store on State Street, where First Federal is today. In fact, she walked everywhere. And, because our education was very important to her, we all graduated from Central High School."

Addrena Mathews Squires, daughter

Sweet Potato Pie

"Her dessert specialties were cakes, apple pies, peach cobblers, and this…"

4 sweet potatoes, baked
1/2 cup butter, softened
2 cups sugar
4 eggs
1 teaspoon cinnamon
1/2 teaspoon salt
1 teaspoon nutmeg
1/4 teaspoon cloves
1 2/3 cups evaporated milk
15 marshmallows

Peel potatoes and mash well. Blend in all ingredients except marshmallows. Pour into pie shells. Bake at 350 degrees until firm. Remove from oven and top with marshmallows. Return to oven until marshmallows melt and form a light crust. Makes 2 pies.

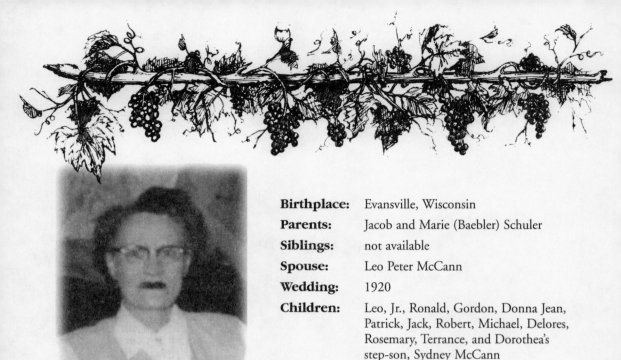

Birthplace: Evansville, Wisconsin

Parents: Jacob and Marie (Baebler) Schuler

Siblings: not available

Spouse: Leo Peter McCann

Wedding: 1920

Children: Leo, Jr., Ronald, Gordon, Donna Jean, Patrick, Jack, Robert, Michael, Delores, Rosemary, Terrance, and Dorothea's step-son, Sydney McCann

Dorothea Schuler McCann
November 18, 1900 – May 7, 1970

During the 1920s, the McCann's lived in the second floor apartment at 720 Mound Street, sharing the house with Mrs. Fannie Schmedemenn who lived on the first floor. Dorothea McCann is described as being "fair-complected with hazel eyes and dark brown hair." She is also described by her children as being "wonderful and very patient and understanding," a virtue that made it possible for the children to be raised in the Catholic Church, like their father, and not Methodist as she was raised. Despite the often crowded conditions in the McCann household, Dorothea always made sure there was room for Terrance, Bernard and Charles McCann, the children's uncles, when they needed a place to stay.

"...needless to say, Ma wore an apron most of the day, maybe because it seemed that she cooked all day long. Vitale's taught her how to make the best Italian spaghetti you ever tasted. To serve with it was a portion of the six loaves of bread she baked every third day. Another specialty was Swiss pear bread. We called it Biera Brot. Aside from the cooking, and everything else on her mind, Ma always had time to sit and listen to what we had to say. I don't remember either Ma or Dad ever having to discipline us. If they did, it probably meant a curfew. When we were little, Christmas was spent at our maternal grandparent's farm in Oregon. Dad had a black buick touring car with shades. Ma always sat in the front seat with him. We had two brown and black water spaniels. They must have been Italian 'cause they sure loved Ma's spaghetti."

Gordon McCann, son

Biera Brot

*"During World War II, Ma substituted prunes for dried pears. Either way,
it is delicious warm from the oven, spread with butter, or toasted the next day."*

4 pounds unpitted prunes
2 1/2 cups of sugar
6 pounds, or more, of flour
2 large cakes of yeast (1 pound)
1 cup warm water
2 tablespoons salt
2 boxes of raisins
2 2.3-ounce bottles of Spice Island anise seed,
    ground in blender until powder-like
2 pounds of walnuts. coarsely chopped

Cook prunes in water to cover with 2 1/2 cups of sugar, saving juice and adding enough water to make a quart (be careful of amount of liquid used later.) Cool; then remove prune pits. Put flour in large bowl. Make a well in center of flour leaving flour banked around sides of bowl. Crumble yeast in well, and mix in 1 cup warm water to form sponge. Let rise one hour. Add prunes and liquid, salt, raisins, anise seed and nuts. Mix well; turn out on table and knead until well combined. Put in warm room and let rise about 1 1/2 hours. Make loaves by cutting dough, kneading into loaf shapes and placing in greased bread pans, making 2 slashes on top of each loaf. Let rise again 1 1/2 hours. Bake at 350 degrees for about 1 hour, or until done. Makes 10 loaves.

Delores McCann Vigdal and Rosemary McCann Leonhardt, daughters

Birthplace: Passo di Rigano, Sicily
Parents: names unavailable, Passo di Rigano, Sicily
Siblings: James, Joseph, Michael, and Anna
Spouse: Alfonso Messina, Palermo, Sicily
Wedding: Passo di Rigano, Sicily
Children: Rosa, Caroline, Marie, and Augustino

Petrina Vitale Messina
1874 – 1959

℘etrina and Alphonse Messina came to this country in 1912 to settle in St. Paul, Minnesota where they became proprietors of a small grocery store. Jim Caruso, who resided in Madison as a partner with Louis Cohn in the Cohn Clothing store on W. Washington Ave., was visiting his brother, Michael, in St. Paul, at which time he was introduced to Caroline Vitale. After a brief courtship, arrangements were made for the couple to marry. After returning to Madison to the apartment upstairs of Urso's, Caroline convinced her parents to sell the store in St. Paul and join them in Madison. Alfonso Messina and Jim Caruso became partners in the White Front Grocery store on the corner of Lake and Mound streets. The families would reside together in the adjacent house at 612 Mound St. When Alfonso died in 1936, Jim, Caroline and Mary continued to operate the store with Petrina. Rosa Urso, Concetta Rane, Anna (Nanutsa) Caruso, Mary Vitale, and Mamie Amato helped to fill the void in Petrina's life by visiting the store daily, and sitting on the front porch after supper to chat with their dear friend.

"Nonna sat on the front porch during the summer months and greeted every person who passed by. Although she'd venture out now and then for a ride with my mother, she preferred staying close to home. When we were babies, she rocked us to sleep. She was a very religious person. If bad weather prevented her from attending Mass, she would light many candles and pray at home."

Annette "Toots" Caruso, granddaughter
(daughter of Caroline)

Cazzilli
Italian Potato Patties

"She seldom left the house....Her front porch was her vacation."

**Mashed potatoes (do not use butter
   as it will make potatoes runny)**
Parmesan cheese
Italian bread crumbs
3-4 eggs
Salt and pepper

Mix all ingredients and form patties from mixture. Deep fry until brown.

Note: Amounts of ingredients should be enough to give patties consistency to shape and fry.

Birthplace:	Minsk, Russia
Parents:	Simon and Esther Urkofsky
Siblings:	10 brothers and sisters
Spouse:	Samuel Moskowsky
Wedding:	1904, England
Children:	Arthur, 1905; Harry, 1907; Esther, 1909; Rose, 1911; Irving, 1913; Rachel, 1915; Reva, 1917; Sara, 1919; and Simon, 1924

Ida Urkofsky Moskowsky
1880 – February 14, 1957

*I*da Urkofsky joined Samuel Moskowsky in England where he served as a baker for the Royal Family. In 1910, he left England to join Ida's brothers and became a baker in Milwaukee, Wisconsin. Nine months later, on July 9, 1911, Ida and their four children arrived at Ellis Island on the SS St. Louis. Later, Samuel learned of an opportunity to own his own bakery in Madison. The family moved once again, this time into an empty three-story building at 214 S. Murray St. Before long, the European-style wood-fired oven and hearth at Moskowsky's new Milwaukee Bakery sent out fragrant messages of bread baking to be remembered years later by everyone who lived in the Greenbush neighborhood. The Moskowsky's living quarters on second floor were quite small. However, because of a baker's schedule, the family made due by sleeping in shifts. After Samuel (Moss) Moskowsky died in 1934, Ida kept the bakery in full operation with the help of her children. With their dedication to the bakery and respect for their mother, the Milwaukee Bakery continued supplying bread and other baked items to local restaurants, churches, synagogues, UW dormitories, retail shops and loyal Greenbush customers. Ida retired in the early 1950s.

"Her Yiddish name was 'Haddash,' but I referred to her as my 'Bubbe' (grandmother). 'Bubbe' became my surrogate mother and most influential person in my life. I treasure memories of her. I remember her 'buyer beware' attitude when shopping for meat at the neighborhood kosher markets. Convinced that one of the butchers weighed meat with a heavy finger, she'd threaten to 'take the meat axe' to the scale. On more than one occasion she'd leave the market and march up the street to Shapiro's. If she wanted a chicken, she'd stop by a place near A.J. Sweet's by the railroad tracks. After she hauled the chicken home in a gunny sack, she'd call Rabbi Madnick, the 'shoyket', to come by her house to make the chicken kosher. By the time the chicken was plucked, singed, cooked and eaten, the only thing left was the beak."

Samuel S. Moss, grandson
(son of Reva)

Chicken Soup

"I treasure memories of her."

1 stewing hen
1 teaspoon salt
1 whole onion
1 stalk celery
2 small carrots
3 whole peppercorns
1 bay leaf

Clean and disjoint hen. Cover with cold water. Add salt. Bring to a boil and skim. Add onion, celery and carrots. Cover and cook slowly until chicken is tender. Strain. If soup is too fat, place in pan of cold water until fat congeals; skim fat off the top and serve.

Birthplace:	Mauston, Wisconsin
Parents:	Frank and Mary (Kamke) Hagen, both second generation German ancestry
Siblings:	not available
Spouse:	John (Jack) O'Connor, Irish ancestry, Riverton, Illinois
Wedding:	not available
Children:	James Earl O'Connor, 1917

Edith Hagen O'Connor
December 14, 1896 – November 10, 1977

$\mathcal{E}$dith Hagen O'Connor's grandson remembers the living quarters he shared with his grandmother at 1022 Regent St., in the 1300 block of Mound Street, and first floor of a building on West Washington Avenue with a roofline that resembled a "castle." Known as a boarding house where "hobos," or "tramps," often stopped by in search of food, the "castle's" resident "saint," Edith O'Connor, compassionate of the homeless, filled their requests by wrapping sandwiches in waxed paper before sending them on their way with a smile.

"She worked endless hours as a cook in local restaurants and taverns. I know she'll be remembered by many customers who once frequented Dolly's Restaurant at 1022 Regent Street. Another place was the El Rancho Restaurant, and, of course, her own O'Connor's Cafe on Williamson Street. There has never been anyone who meant as much to me as she did. She and Grandpa and I would sit at the kitchen table and play Canasta and Euchre and have so much fun. She'd chase me around the kitchen, hug me, and then we'd all laugh together."

John P. O'Connor, Sr., grandson

Fruit and Dumplings

"She'd never turn away a hungry person."

Slice salt pork as thin as possible. Take a few pieces and chop fine. Fry crisp and set aside. Put rest of slices in pan of cold water and bring to a boil. Drain at once to remove the salt. Place slices in frying pan; cover and fry until crisp. Drain off fat 2 or 3 times to keep it crisp. Keep warm until dumplings are ready to serve.

Dumplings:
 3 eggs
 1 cup milk
 1/2 teaspoon salt
 2 cups flour
 1 teaspoon baking powder
 fresh fruit

Mix eggs and milk and stir in mixture of dry ingredients. Boil water in a large kettle. Drop a small piece of dough into boiling water. If it breaks apart, add more flour to dough. Drop dough by large spoonfuls into boiling water and boil 10-12 minutes. Drain. Serve with the chopped salt pork and fruit (blueberries, peaches, etc.) over top and salt pork slices on the side. Yield: 3-4 servings.

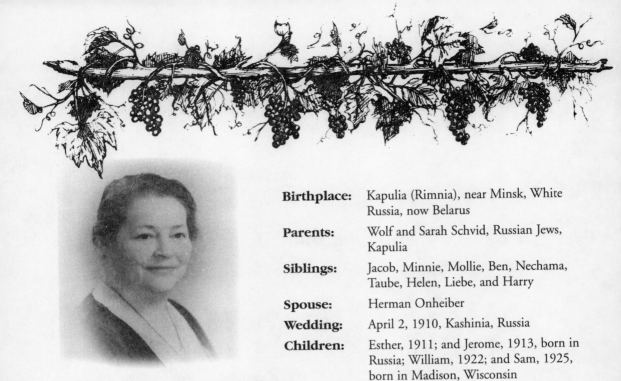

Birthplace:	Kapulia (Rimnia), near Minsk, White Russia, now Belarus
Parents:	Wolf and Sarah Schvid, Russian Jews, Kapulia
Siblings:	Jacob, Minnie, Mollie, Ben, Nechama, Taube, Helen, Liebe, and Harry
Spouse:	Herman Onheiber
Wedding:	April 2, 1910, Kashinia, Russia
Children:	Esther, 1911; and Jerome, 1913, born in Russia; William, 1922; and Sam, 1925, born in Madison, Wisconsin

Bessie Schvid (Sweet) Onheiber
September 19, 1884 – August 1966

*P*ursued by several Russian noblemen, Sarah, instead, chose Herman Schvid to be her husband. Three years later, Schvid would leave Russia, reaching Baltimore in July, 1913, before continuing on to Madison. Forced to wait until after World War I to travel, Bessie, Esther, and Jerome were reunited with Herman in November, 1921. They unpacked their satchels first at 101 S. Park St. before moving to 719 Mound Street. Bessie would remain there after Herman died in 1954 and until the Greenbush neighborhood was razed in 1961. Like many others, she was extremely proud to be in America. The day she became a United State citizen, she stood before the judge, reversing their roles while lecturing to him on the greatness of the country and how people "should get down on their knees and kiss the ground for being fortunate enough to live in America."

"Although we lived on both floors of our two-story house from 1924 to 1932, we rented out one upstairs bedroom. A large porch was added in 1940. There was a small round table and a couch in the front room where Billy and I slept. When he died in 1938, and after World War II, the room was closed off and became my bedroom. I believe our furniture was purchased at one of the second hand stores on W. Washington Ave. It didn't matter. It was home and Mother was very proud of what we had. A very religious woman, she kept three sets of dishes. One for meatless meals, another for meat, and the third set used for Passover. She used to make creamy soup with the heads of perch and bluegills I caught in Lake Monona. It was my dad's favorite. She also loved to visit with neighbors and friends. Mrs. Novick, although born in Russia, was not Jewish, yet visited my mother often to help preserve their Russian language."

Sam Onheiber, son

"She never said an unkind word about anyone, nor was she interested in gossip. When the famous Greenbush gossip expert came by to spread the latest news, Grandma would pretend to be asleep. Sometimes the woman stayed, sat in a chair in Grandma's bedroom, babbling on while Grandma 'slept.'"

Shirley Lewis Wink, granddaughter

Grandma's Stuffing

*"Grandma never wrote down her recipes. One day I wrote
as she prepared her chicken with dressing."*

1 apple, finely chopped
1/2 cup golden raisins
1 egg, beaten
2 level tablespoons cinnamon and sugar combined
   (more cinnamon than sugar)
1/4 level teaspoon salt
Matzo meal, or bread
1 tablespoon melted butter, margarine, or oil
   (hot water if preferred)
Half a chicken

Mix apple, raisins, beaten egg, cinnamon and sugar, and salt together in a bowl and gently stir in matzo meal to make a light fluffy mixture, adding melted butter, or hot water. If using bread, it will take about 5 slices, crumbled to matzo-meal texture. Place chicken on top of stuffing and bake, covered, at 300 degrees for about 1 hour. Apples should be soft and slightly brown.

Birthplace:	Piana degli Albanesi, Sicily
Parents:	John and Mary Cuccia
Siblings:	Nick, Henry, and Anna
Spouse:	Frank Parisi, Piana degli Albanesi, Sicily
Wedding:	1912
Children:	Peter, 1914; Marie, 1916; John, 1920; Angie (Lee) 1922; and George, 1926

Mary Cuccia Parisi
December 24, 1893 – December 23, 1963

*B*y the time Mary Cuccia reached her 12th birthday, she had been spoken for by Frank Parisi. The couple exchanged wedding vows seven years later. Two weeks after the wedding, the newly married couple left their village for America. When they arrived in Madison, they moved in with Mary's sister, Anna Maisano, and her husband, Angelo, who was the proprietor of a neighborhood grocery store. Later, they moved to 1002 Spring Street where their children would be raised.

"The only job my grandmother had outside of the home was as a cook at Jimmy's Spaghetti House on Regent Street, where Josie's is located today. When she learned how to drive, she took many trips to Stoughton. One day, after a farmer ran her off the road, she decided to end her rural excursions. She learned the English language rather quickly even though she continued to speak Albanian in her home. And, of course, she was an excellent cook. I remember how she made fresh noodles and laid them on beds and across chairs to dry. Her hugs were unbelievable, almost taking your breath away."

Terry Parisi, granddaughter
(daughter of George)

"Two wrongs do not make a right" was her favorite expression. She was loving and gentle, strong and hard-working, had many friends and very few enemies, if any at all. She was a natural-born psychologist as she seemed to understand people and always had the right advice to offer...if asked. Yet, she never interfered. And never, ever, gossiped. A truly remarkable woman, mother and friend to all."

Marie Conwell, daughter

Caponatina

"She was devoted to her family..."

2 large eggplant
Olive oil
2 large green pepper, sliced
1 large red pepper, sliced
1 stalk celery, chopped, including leaves
1 large onion, sliced
1 jar pimiento olives
3 cans tomato juice
1 teaspoon basil
1/2 cup brown vinegar
1/2 cup sugar

Peel eggplant and cube. Brown in oil, adding peppers until lightly browned. Steam celery and onion together just slightly and add to rest of vegetables. Drain and rinse olives and add to vegetables. Heat tomato juice with basil. Mix vinegar and sugar together and gradually add to the juice, to taste. Add all vegetables. This can be eaten warm, or chilled, with fresh Italian bread. It keeps well in the refrigerator, and can be processed.

Birthplace:	Piana degli Albanesi, Sicily
Parents:	Demetrio and Philippa (D'avi) Parrino
Siblings:	Vincent, Joseph, Conchera, and Bestiana
Spouse:	Antonio "Pepenini" Parisi
Wedding:	December 8, 1906, St. Demetrios Cathedral, Piana degli Albanesi, Sicily
Children:	Sam, 1907; Demetrio, 1909; Saverio, 1912; Vincent, 1913; Sarah, 1921; Philippa, 1922; Vincent, 1923; Lena, 1925; Conchera, 1926; Joseph, 1927; and Bessie, 1929

Rosaria (Sarah) Parrino Parisi
May 19, 1885 – January 19, 1964

Antonio Parisi, also known as "Pepenini," came to this country in 1914 aboard the vessel, SS Koenig Albert. After working six years to save enough money to send for Rosaria and their four sons, Sam, Demetrio, Saverio, and Vincent, the time finally arrived to be reunited. Rosaria prepared all of the food she and her sons would need for the long journey ahead. Following their departure from Palermo, they were to spend 21 days at sea. They arrived in the New York harbor and Ellis Island on January 2, 1920.

"My fondest memories are of the spaghetti dinners held every Sunday at my nonna's house. After dinner, Nonna would dictate in broken English while my mother wrote letters for her to send to her daughters. Just prior to her death, which happened on a Sunday while hospitalized, she worried about how she was going to make spaghetti for us. Although we continued our Sunday spaghetti dinners after she died, it was never the same. My father made the same sauce, yet something was missing. We tried to figure out if it needed an extra pinch or two of an herb, but later realized it was the love Nonna put into each meal."

Nancy Parisi Denman, granddaughter
(daughter of Vincent)

Italian Sesame Cookies

"Although we continued our Sunday spaghetti dinners after she died, it was never the same."

3 cups flour
1 1/2 cups sugar
1 1/2 teaspoon baking powder
12 tablespoons butter, softened
2 eggs, beaten
3 teaspoons vanilla
1 1/2 cups sesame seeds

Combine flour, sugar and baking powder in large bowl. Blend in butter, vanilla and eggs with wooden spoon. Press dough together with hands. Roll about 1/2 cup dough into a 1-inch rope. Cut into 2-inch lengths. Roll in sesame seeds to coat completely. Arrange cookies about 1/2-inch apart on ungreased baking sheets. Repeat with remaining dough. Bake at 350 degrees until cookies are light brown, about 14 minutes. Cool on racks. Store in airtight container. Makes about 6 dozen.

Birthplace: Bagheria, Sicily

Parents: Batisto and Lorenza (Tutino) Russo

Siblings: Mary, Ben, Anthony, Marian

Spouse: Giuseppi Pellitteri, Bagheria, Sicily

Wedding: July 27, 1913, Chicago, Illinois

Children: Mathew, John, Phil, Frank, Ben, Tony, Frances, Louis, Angelo and Joseph

Maddalena Russo Pellitteri
February, 1897 - 1967

*M*addalena Russo left Sicily with her father on May 12, 1912 to settle in Chicago in a neighborhood with others from Bagheria. Although she was only 15 years old at the time, Maddalena was expected to keep house for her father while he worked as a baker to save enough money to send for the rest of the family. It was during this time that she first met Giuseppi (Joe) Pellitteri, who was also from Bagheria. When she was 16, the couple eloped. Their first child, Mathew, was born in Chicago. In 1915, they moved to Madison with Joe's brother, Phil, and his wife, Maria. Together they purchased a farm on Fish Hatchery Road, later known as the Bowman Dairy. As the family continued to grow, Joe and Maddalena and their children moved to a home at 619 Milton St. that had been moved from the University Avenue area.

"When Prohibition ended, my parents decided to open a tavern. A liquor license stamped #5 was issued to them by the city of Madison for 'The Fox Den' at 724 W. Washington Avenue. It would be the first place in town to serve free spaghetti dinners. However, the city quickly intervened, explaining to my father that he had to charge money for the meals he served. So he did. He charged one cent per plate and there was nothing the city could do about it. While my father continued to work full time as a stone mason, my mother ran the tavern and continued to do so after his death in 1954. When she turned 60, she purchased a 1951 gray stickshift Chevrolet so she could drive to the cemetery to visit his grave."

Louis Pellitteri, son

Cassata

*"This four part recipe was handed down to all our wives by my mother,
as one of her favorites."*

1/2 cup Crisco
1 1/4 cups sugar
2 eggs
2 1/2 cups cake flour
2 teaspoons baking powder
Pinch of salt
1 cup milk
1/2 teaspoon vanilla

Grease and flour a 9 by 13-inch cake pan. Preheat oven to 350 degrees. Cream shortening, sugar and eggs. Sift flour, salt and baking powder and add to mixture alternately with milk. Add vanilla. Pour into cake pan and bake 30-35 minutes or until cake springs back. Cool.

Filling:	Topping:
8 cups milk	2 Hershey chocolate bars, cut into small pieces
2 cups sugar	1 whole slice pineapple, plus small pieces of pineapple
8 egg yolks	1 whole maraschino cherry, plus small pieces of cherries
12 tablespoons cornstarch	1 cup, or more, of chopped walnuts

Mix all filling ingredients together and cook over a burner at medium low heat stirring constantly until the mixture is thick. Set aside to cool. Leave cake in pan for cutting. Have a large round plate ready to assemble the cassata. Cut the cake into parallel strips approximately 1/2-inch wide. (For convenience of handling, cut the cake along the shorterside). Arrange strips of cake into one layer on the round plate and cover the layer of cake with 1/2 of the filling. Sprinkle 1/2 of the chopped chocolate and 1/2 cup of chopped nuts on the filling. Arrange another layer of cake strips and cover with the remaining filling. Place whole pineapple slice in center of the top layer and the whole cherry in the center of the whole slice of pineapple. Place cut pieces of pineapple and cherries alternately around the edge of the top layer. Place another ring of pieces of pineapple and cherries close to the whole pineapple slice in the center of the cake. Sprinkle the remaining chopped nuts and pieces of chocolate over the entire top layer of cake Place cake in refrigerator before serving to set the filling.

Birthplace:	Russia
Parents:	Solomon and Peshe Sweet, Russia
Siblings:	Jessie was the eighth of twelve children
Spouse:	Sam Pollock
Wedding:	February, 1909 Madison
Children:	Harry, 1909; Clarence, 1912; Russell, 1917; and Shirley, 1923

Jessie Sweet Pollock
February 12, l886 - September 12, 1967

Classes held at the Neighborhood House helped to alleviate some of language barriers that created problems for the immigrants in Greenbush. Learning to speak English was an important ingredient in helping Jessie and others in her family communicate with neighbors from other countries, as well as those who lived beyond the boundaries of Greenbush. A few days after the Sweet family arrived in Madison, Solomon found work for Jessie and a sister in a local shoe factory. Sam Pollock arrived from Russia by way of South Africa where he had joined his brother to learn the bricklaying trade. Later, he traveled to Chicago to be with other family members. After Jessie and Sam were married, they lived in a flat on Mound St. where other immigrants stayed while waiting for their loved ones to arrive from Russia. In 1927 the couple purchased a home at 107 S. Mills Street where they remained for 40 years.

"Friday was cleaning and cooking day. Because my mother was unable to get down on her knees to clean the way she wanted to, some of the Italian women in the neighborhood took turns to come in and help. Mother would fix a wonderful lunch to enjoy together at the kitchen table. She impressed on us the importance of kindness and when the Depression came, we survived by having young Jewish university students stay at our home. Each young man was treated like family and shared good meals with us as our brothers. In the backyard was a grape arbor like those found in our Italian neighbors' yards. My father made Concord wine from the grapes, but Mother concentrated on our cherry tree. Although the cherries were sour, they were canned and lined up with jars of other types of food harvested from the garden. Back then, there were no special food requests for dinner. What was cooked was what you ate...and everyone was expected to enjoy each meal."

Russell Pollock, son

Stuffed Cabbage or Prokes

"Learning to speak English was an ingredient necessary to mainstream the immigrants."

1 large head of cabbage
1/2 cup strained tomatoes
1 large onion
1 tablespoon syrup or honey
2 tablespoons sugar
1/4 teaspoon salt, dash of ginger
1 whole allspice
1 clove
1/2 bay leaf
Juice of 1/2 lemon

Filling:
1 pound chopped raw beef
1 egg
1 tablespoon matzo meal
1/2 onion grated
1 tablespoon water
Dash of salt, pepper and cinnamon
1/2 cup white raisins
Cornstarch for thickening agent

By cutting close to the stem, carefully remove the leaves from a head of cabbage. Place in a large kettle and cover with boiling water for 5 or 10 minutes until they are soft. Drain off water. Mix chopped meat with grated onion, egg, water, matzo meal, and seasoning. One-half cup of cooked rice may be added to the meat, if desired. Fill each leaf with a few raisins and a portion of meat mixture in proportion to its size. Fold over the ends of the leaf and roll. Cut the onion fine and place in a kettle together with tomatoes, lemon juice, sugar, syrup, and seasoning. Now put in cabbage rolls, open end down, add a cup of water and simmer slowly for at least 1 11/2 hours, basting occasionally. Cabbage should be tender and brown. Thicken sauce with a teaspoon of cornstarch mixed with a little cold water, and cook for 10 minutes longer.

Birthplace: Palermo, Sicily

Parents: Antonio and Giuseppina Tumminello

Siblings: Salvatore, John, Rose, and Catherine

Spouse: Frank Prestigiacomo, Palermo, Sicily

Wedding: 1920, Palermo, Sicily

Children: Nick, 1921; Anthony, 1922; Mary, 1924; Joseph, 1926; Sam, 1928; Josephine, 1929; Frank, Jr. 1943

Rose Tumminello Prestigiacomo
March 8, 1899 - December 5, 1992

Rose and Frank Prestigiacomo arrived in Madison as newlyweds on March 4, 1920. They lived at 638 Milton St. until 1925, at which time a home was purchased at 12 South Lake St. It is where they would remain until the 1960s when the city's urban renewal plan forced them to move. Leaving the home they loved was traumatic for them and, although they attempted to fight ejection, they lost as others had. With all their belongings packed, they left the Greenbush neighborhood to settle in an unfamiliar neighborhood.

"My mother was a happy, generous, person who went out of her way to make people happy. Sensing the importance of being involved with our school and church, she attended all PTA meetings and baked bushels of cookies with friends to sell as PTA fund-raisers. She also had great respect for the nuns. Every Halloween she'd bake a huge whipped cream cake, add a half-gallon of ice cream, then had us kids take it to the nuns for "treats." Our kitchen provided great happiness for all of us. We gathered around the table to eat, play cards and bingo, or just to laugh, talk, argue...whatever. Bread was made twice a week, eight loaves each time. Oftentimes, when baking, she'd use the dough for rolls, then stuff each one with ricotta and grated cheese. Mondays always began at 3 a.m. when she'd go down to the cellar to start the laundry. By the time we went downstairs for breakfast, the kitchen was literally bursting with dozens of oatmeal cookies, or a freshly baked chocolate or white sheet cake. She was my inspiration. I, too, love to cook and bake and owe it all to her."

Mary Prestigiacomo Maiale, daughter

Vastati

"Similar to calzone, this is what my mother used to make on the Feast of the Immaculate Conception. The only significance I know of making vastati on December 8th is that it was a tradition in her native Palermo..."

6 homemade rolls (can use frozen bread dough)
ricotta cheese
shredded Romano cheese
olive oil
pepper to taste

Split freshly baked warm buns. Layer, to your liking, amounts of ricotta, shredded cheese, olive oil, and black pepper. They should be eaten while still warm.

Birthplace:	Russia
Parents:	Hirsh and Alta Perlstein
Siblings:	Abraham, Jake, David, Alex and Sophie
Spouse:	Harry Sweet
Wedding:	1914
Children:	Leonard and Sylvan Sweet Phyllis Prosansky

Anna Perlstein Sweet Prosansky
1894 - 1984

*A*nna and Harry's travels continued after arriving in America when they moved west to Wisconsin and the Greenbush neighborhood in Madison. In 1918, Harry died during the flu epidemic. Anna struggled as a 20-year-old widow with a 2 1/2 year old child and a six month old infant. Described as "fiercely proud and independent," she supported her family as a seamstress. Her modest home on Mound St. became a boarding house for University of Wisconsin students who desired Kosher meals. In 1923, Anna married Meyer Prosansky, a widower with two sons, Milton and Sydney. In 1930, Anna gave birth to a daughter, Phyllis. Other Prosansky addresses in the neighborhood included 205 S. Park St., and in the 1930s, 217 S. Mills St.

"It seemed that she worked all the time. I remember coming home from school to discover freshly baked breads, chocolate cakes, and supper cooking in the oven. The aroma was mouth-watering. She never bought bread. Everything was homemade. She became very popular with my friends, as well as with her own friends, because of her baking. During summer evenings, when we lived on S. Mills St., we'd sit on the screened porch and sing. She had a lovely voice and an incredible memory of songs and lyrics, many of which I am sure were learned phonetically."

Phyllis Prosansky Lefcowitz, daughter

Puter Kuchen (Sweet Rolls)

"She never used recipes, but my daughter, Dale, made certain this, one of our favorites, was recorded..."

3 cups of flour
1 ounce cake yeast
1/4 cup lukewarm water
1 stick melted butter
1/2 cup sugar
3/4 cup warmed milk
2 eggs
Cinnamon and sugar

Bring all ingredients to room temperature. Sift flour; make a well in the flour. Crumble in cake yeast. Add lukewarm water and mix. Mix together melted butter, sugar and warmed milk. Add to flour mixture. Add 2 eggs; knead. Dough should not be too sticky. Let rise.

Cut into 3 sections. Roll out each section, spread with butter and sprinkle with cinnamon and sugar. Roll into loaves and cut across to form rolls. Let rise again. Bake at 350 degrees for 25-30 minutes.

Birthplace: Palermo, Sicily

Parents: Frank and Teresa Lo CoCo, Passo di Rigano, Sicily

Siblings: Teresa, Josephine, and Francesca

Spouse: Joseph Puccio, Messina, Sicily

Wedding: 1911, Palermo, Sicily

Children: Charles, Jack, Paul, Jeni, and Lilly

Maria Lo CoCo Puccio
1888 - 1971

*P*uccio's arrived in Madison in 1912 and lived at 788 West Washington Avenue. The kitchen in the two-story house is described as being large and "very Italian" with a round table where all meals were served. Morning duties for Maria began with cleaning their bar, Puccio's Tavern, which was adjacent to their house. By noontime, when she had finished her chores, she'd visit Troia's Market to purchase what was planned for the evening meal. Her daily "quiet time" arrived about 2 p.m. when washing, ironing and cleaning was done. After resting a while, she'd begin food preparation for their 6 o'clock supper.

"Ma always had a smile on her face. She was a happy person with a beautiful voice and sang Italian songs with everything she did. Although the curtains in the house were made of white lace, I remember her favorite color being a light blue. She was proud of our place on West Washington Ave. and was an immaculate housekeeper. She was also a great cook. Some of her favorites were spiedini, fried or stuffed artichokes, minestrone, veal stew, and a sweet and sour halibut that I was particularly fond of. If we went shopping together, we'd usually stop at Woolworth's Dime Store for lunch. If there was time, we'd take in a movie before returning home. She was a wonderful mother."

Jeni Puccio Traino, daughter

Italian Roast Loin of Pork with Potatoes

"She was a great cook, too. With spiedini, fried or stuffed artichokes, minestrone and veal stew, this was another one of our favorites."

3-4 pound pork loin roast
1/4 cup oil
Salt to taste
1/2 teaspoon pepper
1/4 teaspoon oregano
2 garlic cloves, minced
3 sprigs fresh parsley, chopped
2 cups water
6 potatoes, cut in half

Rub pork with oil. Season with salt, pepper, oregano and garlic. Place in roasting pan. Roast in 350 degree oven for 2 1/2 hours or until done. One hour before roast is done, add water and potatoes. Baste often, adding more seasonings to your taste.

Birthplace:	San Giuseppe Iato, Sicily
Parents:	Giuseppe and Martha Coniglio
Siblings:	a sister, Nicolina, and one brother
Spouse:	Antonio Joseph Pullara, San Giuseppe Iato, Sicily
Wedding:	San Giuseppe Iato, Sicily
Children:	Caspar, 1891; Mary, 1897; Jack, 1894; Ann; and Lilly, 1898 were Antonio's children. Felicia and Antonio's children were Joseph, 1907, and John, 1913, both born in San Giuseppe; and Leonard, 1925, born in Madison, Wisconsin

Felicia Coniglio Pullara
October 18, 1884 - May 18, 1976

Caspar traveled alone from Palermo and in 1913, after working two jobs in America, sent for the rest of the family. They lived on Spring St., then moved to N. Murray St. behind DiSalvo's store. In the 1920s, they moved across Regent St. to 5 S. Murray St., next to Gervasi's store. Though a strong-willed family disciplinarian, Felicia became ill with tuberculosis and was hospitalized in Wales, near Milwaukee. Joe and John were temporarily placed in Milwaukee's St. Francis orphanage. Later, while recuperating in Madison, Felicia decided to visit her little boys and traveled alone with a note asking for help if she become lost. Needing assistance, she approached a woman sweeping her front steps. Being of Irish ancestry, the woman read the note and directed Felicia to the orphanage. For the rest of her life, Felicia Pullara had great respect for the Irish. Pullara's S. Murray Street address resembled a tiny farm house in the middle of the city. Chickens laid eggs in the backyard, and a goat was kept for milking. In the kitchen, behind cabinet glass doors, coffee cups hid pignola, and the coal burning stove, their only source of heat, placed in the center of the room, toasted buttered bread on a ridge that hugged the stove's base.

"Tomatoes were dried each summer on a board set up along the side of the house. While her garden provided vegetables, the grapevine bore fruit and offered cool shade during the warm summer months. In the evenings, Mrs. Gervasi, Mrs. Pellitteri, Mrs. DiSalvo, Mrs. Corona, and Mrs. Provenzano gathered on their porches to chat while snapping peas and beans. It was a wonderful neighborhood. Although Grandma didn't have a driver's license and never had driven a car, she sat behind the steering wheel one day of a touring Model "T" that belonged to her cousin Momena Manino's deceased husband, and drove Momena to the cemetery to visit his grave."

Phyllis Pullara Olson, granddaughter
(daughter of Joe)

Iretta Pullara,
(wife of Joe's son, Tony)

Cardune, Pullara-style

"An early Spring Sicilian ritual..."

Cardune, or burdock, should be picked in early spring during a period of tenderness. Pull each stalk from head and remove any stringy parts. Wash under running water using a vegetable brush. Add juice from half of a fresh lemon to boiling water. Add salt to taste. Lower cardune into boiling water with enough water to cover. Cook until tender, but do not over cook. Drain. Pat dry with paper towels and cut stalks in half.

Bread crumb mixture:
2 garlic cloves, finely chopped
1 medium onion, chopped
1 2-ounce can anchovies in oil
2 cups bread crumbs
Salt and pepper to taste
1/2 cup grated Romano cheese

Sauté garlic and onions in small amount of oil. Add anchovies, stirring and mashing while heating. Slowly stir in bread crumbs and season. Cook on low heat, stirring until crumbs are light brown. Remove from heat. Add Romano cheese and mix well. Lay 3 or 4 stalks of cooked cardune on flat surface. Spread each stalk with crumb mixture. Place cardune together so crumb mixture is inside as a stuffing. Tie together with white store string. Fry tied cardunes in pan with about 1/4-inch of oil. Turn and brown lightly

Birthplace:	Madison, Wisconsin
Parents:	Andrew and Catherine Hobbes Kinney, "Yankee" and Irish
Siblings:	Jennie, Nellie, Ed (Harriett's twin), Andy, Lil, Alice, Grace, Jess, and Jo
Spouse:	Timothy Quinlan, Ireland
Wedding:	1892
Children:	Edward, 1894; Mary, 1896; and Margaret, 1897

Harriet Kinney Quinlan
1874 - date of death unknown
(Mary and Margaret Quinlan, 1900)

*I*t is believed that Harriet Kinney's mother was born in Madison sometime during the 1850s. Harriet's father, born in 1841, arrived in Madison by way of Canada and fought in the Civil War from 1861 to 1865. Catherine and Andrew Kinney raised their family at 432 West Doty Street. Harriet and Timothy Quinlan lived at 140 Proudfit Street in a house embraced by a large porch. The kitchen, similar to others during that time, had a sink pump. Stored on shelves in the pantry were Ball jars filled with preserves and other homegrown nourishment from the garden. As a devout Catholic and lifelong parishioner at St. Raphael's Cathedral, Harriet had been described to her grandson as a beautiful woman with large, deep-set, violet-blue eyes. A favorite family story claims that Harriet witnessed the face of a full moon surfacing from the depths of Lake Monona as she walked one evening along the shores of Brittingham Park.

"There was always plenty of canning going on in our house. One hot August day I ran inside through the back screen door for a cool drink to quench my thirst. As a three year old, I wasn't paying attention to anything until I fell into the fruit cellar through a door opened to accommodate canners engaged in putting up a relish they called "Chicago Hot." Because the floor was dirt, instead of cement, I survived. So did the canning party. While the Italians were gorging themselves on delicious pasta dishes swimming in rich delicious sauces, the Irish depression staple was a cold tomato, 20 cents worth of hamburger, and a potato. We just never caught on to the idea that soup and sauce needed a meat base of some kind. And, while magnificent crusty homemade Italian bread was layered with cotto salami and mortadella, our sandwiches, made with Gardner's cheapest white bread, were spread with mayonnaise relish. Sometimes we'd strike it rich by adding a piece of tuna fish."

James A. Ripp, grandson

Boxty

"When I was a kid, I remember hearing tales from an old Irish crone, a face full of wrinkles, smoking her clay pipe beside a wood stove, taking a wee nip once in a while for her cold bones. She knew everybody in town; where and how they lived Out of envy for theirs, or maybe excessive pride in her own situation, when asked where so-and-so lived, she would respond with a pejorative and a bit of spittle, "out among the bushes t'other side of the tracks."

1 pound of potatoes
6 ounces of flour
1/4 pint fresh milk
1 1/2 teaspoon salt
1 1/2 teaspoon baking powder

Peel and grate raw potatoes. Add flour, salt, milk in this order, followed with baking powder. Mix well. Drop tablespoons of mixture on hot greased pan. Cook slowly until thoroughly cooked and golden brown color on both sides. Butter while hot and serve on a dish with a paper doily underneath.

Birthplace: Piana degli Albanesi, Sicily

Parents: Frank and Josephine (Mandala) Salerno

Siblings: Rose, George, Tony and Lawrence

Spouse: John Baptist Raimondo, San Cipirello, Sicily

Wedding: July 22, 1922, St. Joseph Catholic Church, Madison, Wisconsin

Children: Vincella, 1924; and Josephine, 1931

Conchera Salerno Raimond
December 12, 1905 - March 7, 1996

Conchera Salerno was only three years old when her family came to this country. After living in the Greenbush neighborhood for fourteen years, she and John Raimondo were married. Their home at 914 College Court was just a few blocks away from 1213 Regent St. where John's shoe repair business was located.

"My mother's days were very much like what others experienced. She loved to cook and made delicious bread, pizza and many other Italian dishes. The many memorable times we had together include picnics, camping, and cookouts in the backyard. If she was tired, she'd rest on the daven-port. Because she was a wonderful mother, we, in turn, have wonderful memories to last a lifetime."

Vincella Raimond Krause, daughter

Breaded Sirloin Steak

"Picnics at Hoyt Park were very special for all of us..."

1 pound sirloin steak, sliced thin
Olive oil
Bread crumbs
Grated Italian cheese

Dip sirloin steak in olive oil, then coat with mixture of bread crumbs and grated Parmesan or Romano cheese. Broil until golden brown and crispy on one side. Turn once to repeat the process.

Note: Italian seasoned bread crumbs can be used as a substitute for crumbs and grated cheese. Steak can be dipped in an egg wash of egg and milk before coating with crumbs if prepared indoors in a fry pan.

Birthplace:	San Cipirello, Sicily
Parents:	John Battista Terrazi and Rosa (Polizzi) Terrazi
Siblings:	not available
Spouse:	Salvatore Raimondo
Wedding:	November, 1894, San Cipirello, Sicily
Children:	Antonio, 1895; Lucia, 1897; John, 1900; Rose 1902; Anna, 1906; Joseph, 1910; Mary, 1914; and Providence, 1916

Vincenza Terrazi Raimondo
December 29, 1873 - September, 1972

Salvatore Raimondo left San Cipirello, Sicily for New Orleans in 1910 to work and save money before returning home. The second time he sailed for America his plans were to settle in Madison where village friends had already gathered. In 1912, his oldest son, Antonio, would join him there. The following year, Vincenza and their five remaining children left home to be reunited as a family. They resided at a Regent St. location for a few months before moving to a seven room home they purchased for $2,400 and had moved to 10 N. Murray St. The 50-year old home had been scheduled for razing near the Capitol Square. It was one of many dwellings moved to the Greenbush plat to provide living quarters for the arriving immigrants. With a little money down and interest paid twice a year, the Raimondo's were introduced to the American dream. A spacious lower level of the home served as a kitchen where a large wood burning cookstove and a potbellied stove heated the entire two-story structure. It was there where family gathered each Sunday and on holidays to enjoy Sicilian food, homemade bread, wine from backyard grapevines, and music played by family members. Although money was not in abundance in the Raimondo household, their outlook on everything was optimistic while great importance was placed on their children's education.

"Monday was wash day. Tuesday she ironed. Mending was done on Wednesday, and Thursday was set aside for light cleaning. Heavier cleaning took place Friday and Saturday. Even though Sunday was a day of 'rest,' she cooked for hours. Yet, there was always time for her to do beautiful needlework and teach those skills to her daughters. Mama Grande took great delight in doing her jobs well so there was extra time to spend in her garden. She was a very loving person who demanded respect, and got it. When the neighborhood was destroyed during the 1960s, she refused to leave her home until a date had been set to tear it down."

Teresa Raimondo Small, granddaughter
(daughter of Antonio)

Pasta Minestra

"This was daily basic fare, with variations, of course, depending on the garden greens available, like tenterumi, the tender leaves and tendrils of the Sicilian squash we call cucuzza."

1 small onion
Fresh tomatoes, or 1 16-ounce can of whole tomatoes
Vegetables, such as peas, spinach, Swiss chard,
       asparagus, zucchini, or beans
Basil
Parsley
Water, as necessary
Salt and pepper
1 pound of pasta of your choice
Grated Parmesan or Romano cheese

Sauté a medium chopped onion in olive oil. Break up tomatoes into onions. Add vegetables of your choice, chopped basil and parsley, water, and salt and pepper. When tender, add this mixture to cooked pasta. Serve with grated cheese.

Birthplace:	Cammarata, Sicily
Parents:	Salvatore and Antoinette (Mastrella) Bongiovani
Siblings:	Vincenza, Carmella, Angelina, Joseph, Gaetano, and Salvatore
Spouse:	Giuseppe Reina, Cammarata, Sicily
Wedding:	1901, Cammarata, Sicily
Children:	Sam, 1903; James, 1906; John, 1914; Anthony, 1916; Mayme; and Frank, 1922

Concetta Bongiovani Reina (Rane)
September 8, 1883 - October, 1957

Giuseppe Reina came to America following the birth of his second son, James. By the time he departed from New York for Wisconsin, his name, misspelled as Rane by authorities at Ellis Island, had been innocently accepted as his new American name. In 1912, Concetta left Sicily with Sam and James to establish a new home with Giuseppe at 612 Milton St. She is described as being very loving and protective, cheerful and optimistic. Widowed at age 50, she supervised and maintained family unity and harmony. When her health failed in later years, her thoughts remained centered on her family and their future.

"No one ever went hungry at a table set by my mother. Her senses and imagination produced culinary masterpieces. Humming and singing in the kitchen attested to her love of doing for her family and guests. On bread-baking day, she always made two tiny loaves for me to have when I arrived home from school at St. Joe's. She'd slice a loaf in half, rub it with oil, then sprinkle it with grated cheese. I also remember how much she loved to walk uptown to browse through stores on the Square before stopping at Kresge's Five and Dime for one of their famous hot dogs and cold root beers. If there was time, she'd walk over to the Majestic Theater on King St. to see a movie and receive a piece of dishware for attending the matinee. She collected enough to furnish us with two complete sets of dishes. After my father died, she made certain tradition continued. We were young at the time, but we all attended midnight Mass on Christmas Eve, then returned home to grilled Italian sausage, salad, anise, seafood, wine, breads and her own version of pizza covered with crushed tomatoes, anchovies and a special sprinkling of spices and herbs."

Frank J. Rane, son

Pollo Stufata con Pomodoro e Patata
Baked Chicken with Tomato and Potato

"...and as hard as I try to duplicate her cooking skills, I still haven't achieved quite the same flavors I remember so well, but this is close..."

1 3/4 pound fryer chicken, cut up in 10 pieces
Flour
Salt and Pepper to taste
1/2 cup olive oil
3-4 garlic cloves, chopped (more or less, according to taste)
1 28-ounce can of crushed tomatoes
5-6 fresh basil leaves, or 1 teaspoon dry basil, more or less
1 teaspoon, more or less, or oregano, or to taste
4 medium potatoes, peeled and quartered
1 medium onion, cut in half, lengthwise, and sliced thin
1 8-ounce can of peas, drained
Grated Parmesan or Romano cheese

Dredge chicken in seasoned flour. Brown in olive oil in skillet; remove and set aside. Drain off any excess oil leaving just enough to sauté garlic and onion until soft. Add tomatoes, mashing large pieces, and simmer for a few minutes. Add basil and oregano and simmer a few minutes more and set aside.

Use a broiler pan and arrange chicken in single layer, skin side up. Place quartered potatoes between chicken pieces. Pour tomato sauce over chicken and potatoes making sure a little of the sauce goes under the chicken. Cover with foil and bake in a preheated 375 degree oven for about 45 to 50 minutes. Remove foil and distribute the drained peas over chicken mixture making sure peas are pressed into the sauce. Sprinkle cheese lightly over entire mixture and bake another 10 to 15 minutes. Test for tenderness. Add additional salt and pepper to your own taste.

Note: A pan other than a broiler pan can be used that will hold chicken and potatoes in a single layer.

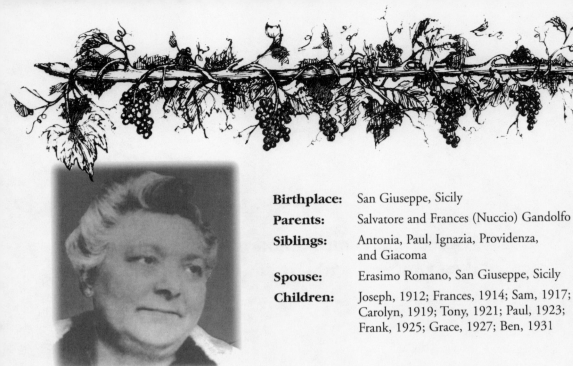

Birthplace: San Giuseppe, Sicily

Parents: Salvatore and Frances (Nuccio) Gandolfo

Siblings: Antonia, Paul, Ignazia, Providenza, and Giacoma

Spouse: Erasimo Romano, San Giuseppe, Sicily

Children: Joseph, 1912; Frances, 1914; Sam, 1917; Carolyn, 1919; Tony, 1921; Paul, 1923; Frank, 1925; Grace, 1927; Ben, 1931

Maria Gandolfo Romano
December 20, 1888 - April 4, 1945

A year after Erasimo Romano arrived here in 1910, having been sponsored by local contractor T. W. Quinn, and local mason Paul Corona, his wife, Maria, sailed into the New York harbor with expectations that her husband would be there, as planned, to greet her. To her dismay, she found herself alone. And to add to the confusion, authorities began making plans for her return to Sicily within 24 hours. When Erasimo was contacted in Madison he, too, was confused and shocked as he was expecting her boat to arrive on a different date. He left immediately for New York to claim his young bride.

"When you entered the front door there was the unmistakable aroma of baked bread and tomato sauce. My brother, Paul, was an outstanding athlete and football player at Central High. His good friends and Black team buddies Ed Withers, Isiah Carthron, and Chuck Collins, were also from the neighborhood. They ate many meals at our house. They didn't have any choice. My mother wouldn't let them leave without eating. That was typical of the togetherness in the old Greenbush neighborhood. My mother was kind, gentle, loved everyone, and was loved by all. When she died of a heart attack at age 54, it was a great loss to everyone."

Frank Romano, son

Schiachatta

"She was an excellent cook who never wrote down a single recipe."

Homemade or frozen bread dough
Canned anchovies
1 16-ounce can of whole tomatoes
Chopped onions
1 tablespoon, more or less, of dried oregano
Grated Parmesan cheese

Press dough to about 1/4-inch thickness in a long cookie sheet with sides. Chop anchovies in pieces and press deeply into dough about 1-inch apart. With hands, squeeze juice from each tomato over dough, then tear tomatoes into pieces to distribute over dough. Save juice from can to use in another recipe. Sprinkle with chopped onions, oregano and grated Parmesan. Place in a 375 degree oven and bake for about 20 minutes.

Birthplace: Palermo, Sicily

Parents: John and Josephine (Guidera) Licali, Piana degli Albanesi, Sicily

Siblings: Dominic, George, Mary, Elizabeth, and Ninfa

Spouse: George Salerno, Piana degli Albanesi, Sicily

Wedding: 1909, New Orleans, Louisiana

Children: Frank, Vito, John, Josephine, and Rose

Victoria Licali Salerno
December 16, 1893 - September 27, 1981

Victoria Licali accompanied her three sisters and their widowed mother to this country sometime around 1908 and settled in New Orleans where her brothers had arrived earlier to work the sugar plantation fields. While residing there, George Salerno took a fancy to Victoria and serenaded her in the evening beneath her window. He continued until she promised the two would someday wed. After their wedding, they moved to Madison and lived next door to the Capadona family at Park and Regent streets. Their next move was to 1006 Spring St. where the family would remain. Members of the Salerno family exuded talent. George and his brothers, Tony and Lawrence, were accomplished musicians as were George and Victoria's sons, Frank, Vito and John. The Spring St. address became a gathering spot for parties and street dances. Because Victoria had attended school in Sicily, she was one of few in the neighborhood with Italian reading and writing skills. She was often called on by friends to translate letters they had received from home. By attending reading and writing classes at Neighborhood House, she also learned to communicate in English. She loved children and when the weather was pleasant, she and friends would pack wagons with little ones and plenty of food for long walks to Vilas Park for afternoon picnics.

"There was always excitement at my grandmother's house. One night, my grandfather arrived home with news that he had been given a car as payment for performing with the Joe Tantillo Band. It was the first vehicle he had ever owned and wanted to take his family for a ride. Although she protested, my pajama-clad grandmother and the children climbed into the Model T and headed for Vilas Park where the car rolled down a hill and got stuck in the lagoon. My grandmother huddled in the car, embarrassed, trying to hide her nightgown with a coat, while the pajama-clad children laughed with glee. Grandpa had to leave them to call his brother for help. It was the first and last car for the Salerno family."

Carolyn Cuccia Bonanno, granddaughter
(daughter of Josephine)

Cauliflower Omelet, Sicilian-style

"When my grandpa and uncles entertained on Spring St., my grandmother concentrated on her needlework, storytelling, baking crusty loaves of Italian bread, and preparing authentic Sicilian dishes like this..."

1 medium to large cauliflower, chopped
Salt and pepper to taste
2 tablespoons oil
1/3 - 2/3 cup Italian-style bread crumbs
2 eggs, beaten
1/2 cup grated Parmesan cheese
1/4 cup Italian-style bread crumbs

Cook cauliflower until almost tender; salt and pepper to taste. After heating oil in Teflon frying pan, sprinkle seasoned bread crumbs onto oil and lightly brown. In a bowl, using a fork, coarsely mash together cauliflower and two eggs. Add grated cheese and additional 1/4 cup; mix together. Put cauliflower mixture in pan on top of bread crumbs. Over medium heat, brown for about 3 minutes, then turn over and brown on the other side. Turn over with a plate and serve.

Note: If an omelet pan is used, half of cauliflower mixture is poured into pan and cooked, adding additional oil and bread crumbs when cooking the remaining mixture.

Birthplace:	Piana degli Albanesi, Sicily
Parents:	John and Josephine (Guidera) Licali:
Siblings:	Dominic, George, Mary, Elizabeth, Victoria, and Ninfa
Spouse:	Giorgio Scalissi, Piana degli Albanesi, Sicily
Wedding:	November 4, 1906, St.Louis Cathedral, New Orleans, Louisiana
Children:	Mary, 1907; Joseph, 1909; John, 1911; Josephine, 1913; Fanny, 1915; Vito, 1919; Ted, 1922; Ninfa, 1923; Sally, 1926; Betty, 1932; and George, 1935

Elizabeth Licali Scalissi
February 22, 1888 - July 3, 1976

*E*lizabeth's brothers, Dominic and George, sailed together for New Orleans and worked the sugar cane fields until they had saved $10.00 per person, "open" boat passage, for their sisters and widowed mother, Josephine. George would remain in New Orleans for a period of time before leaving for Madison to find work and be reunited with friends and family members already settled there. Elizabeth, also known as "Tukya," married Giorgio Scalissi in the St. Louis Cathedral in New Orleans. When plans were finalized for the family to join George in Madison, they said goodbye to Dominic who chose to remain in Louisiana. The three-story dwelling in Greenbush at 824 Regent St., where all 11 Scalissi children were raised, had a living room, large kitchen, and two bedrooms on the first floor. During the summer months, the youngsters slept on the front and back porches.

"A typical day for my mother was to care for all of us, tend to her backyard garden and grapevines, visit the store at least twice, chat with neighbors along the way, and bake bread, soup and stews."

Sally Scalissi Ward, daughter

"You could say she was a typical Italian mother. She lived vicariously for her children. They were her life and, in return, they deeply loved her. In fact, as adults, many of them moved into the apartments in the family home so they could remain together. It was, in essence, the Italian-way. Nonna was a Charter member of the Italian Women's Club and enjoyed attending evening meetings held at the clubhouse just a half block away. Years following the death of her husband, she married George Giusti, a founding member of the Italian Workmen's Club."

Rossario G. Parisi, grandson
(son of Mary)

Chicken, Scalissi-style

"Although my mother seldom used anything other than bay leaves to season food, basil or other favorite herbs can be added to complement it's nice flavor..."

1 3-pound whole chicken, cut up
5 medium potatoes, peeled and left whole
1 medium onion, cut in small pieces
4-5 carrots, cut lengthwise
1 can of peas, drained, saving liquid
Salt and pepper to taste
Basil, optional

Put chicken in medium size roaster or baking dish and place potatoes, onions and carrots around the chicken. Add liquid from peas, and seasonings, and bake 1 hour at 350 degrees. Thirty minutes before chicken is done, add peas. Delicious with homemade bread.

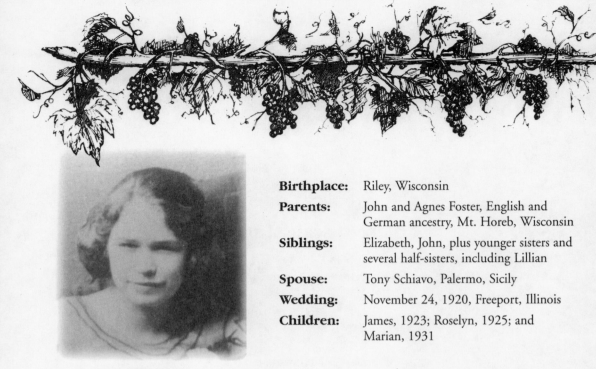

Birthplace:	Riley, Wisconsin
Parents:	John and Agnes Foster, English and German ancestry, Mt. Horeb, Wisconsin
Siblings:	Elizabeth, John, plus younger sisters and several half-sisters, including Lillian
Spouse:	Tony Schiavo, Palermo, Sicily
Wedding:	November 24, 1920, Freeport, Illinois
Children:	James, 1923; Roselyn, 1925; and Marian, 1931

Celia Foster Schiavo
October 18, 1905 -

Celia Foster, described as being very mature for her age, was 15 years old when she married Tony Schiavo. After their elopement, the newlyweds moved to the third floor apartment of Mrs. Capitani's house at 5 S. Frances Street. Later, they would build a home a few doors away at 1 S. Frances. When their Stone Front Tavern was built in front of the house, the address would change to 531 and 533 Regent St. Although Celia was determined to finish high school, and attended the University of Wisconsin, she was forced to discontinue her studies to raise their children.

"In her earlier years, my mother and her older sister, Elizabeth, worked at a supermarket on State Street. Elizabeth was married then and introduced my mother to Tony Schiavo. Because my father was 12-years older than my mother, we often laughed at his comments that my mother married him for his money since he had a total of only $50.00 in his pocket at the time. My mother couldn't cook when they first married and, although she was an immaculate housekeeper, she had a way of messing up the kitchen while preparing a meal. It was my job to keep things in order. In later years, she would spend time with the Amato offspring when babies were born. She has been a loving, caring mother and grandmother who always put her family first."

Marian Schiavo Skille, daughter

Navy Bean and Ham Soup

*"She couldn't boil water when she first got married. I remember
her saying she once cooked 3 pounds of beans for an average recipe and had
every pan in the house filled to the brim..."*

1 pound dry navy beans
2 quarts of cold water
1 meaty ham bone
1/2 teaspoon baking soda
1/2 teaspoon salt
1 1/2 teaspoon pepper, or to taste
2 bay leaves
2 medium onions, diced
1 fresh tomato, cut in small pieces

Rinse beans and place in a 6 quart kettle with cold water and 1/2 teaspoon baking soda.
The next morning, without draining, add ham bone, seasonings and bring to boil. Cover,
reduce heat and simmer about 3 hours. Stir occasionally. Remove bone, cut off meat and
dice. Return meat to soup. Add onions and tomato and simmer about 45 minutes.
Delicious with homemade bread. Serves about 8 people.

Birthplace: New Orleans, Louisiana

Parents: George and Mary (Colletti) Renda, Piana degli Albanesi, Sicily

Siblings: Angeline and Ben

Spouse: Joseph Schiro

Wedding: September 2, 1917, St. Joseph's Catholic Church, Madison, Wisconsin

Children: Frank, George, Mary, Frank, George and Damian

Catherine Renda Schiro
October 31, 1900 - September 14, 1946

Catherine, or "Katie," Renda was eight years old when her family moved to Madison. She remembered her father telling of his early arrival in New Orleans, and serving in the Spanish American War in 1898. When the family left Louisiana, it was to join George's brothers, Joe and Sam, who had already settled in Madison with tales of their first winter when they slept in an unheated attic of a house near Union Corners, on Madison's eastside. Much later, when Catherine married Joe Schiro, the newlyweds moved to a three-flat at 811 Regent St. owned by Joe's brother, Pete, and his wife, Angeline (Catherine's sister...two brothers married two sisters). The two families lived together for about ten years, during which time the children were born. Later, Catherine and Joe moved to 909 College Court, and in 1940, moved once again, this time to living quarters on the second floor of their business, Schiro's Tavern, located on the corner of Regent and S. Brooks streets.

"One day, when Ma and Pa were courting, with Nonna present to keep things 'proper,' they went for a walk. Ma fell down and Nonna 'commanded' Pa to help her up. Pa refused, stating that it was 'against the rules' to touch her. Nonna stayed mad at Pa forever. A short time after Ma's fall, Nonna took ill and thought she was about to, as Pa described a fatal illness, 'cash in her chips.' Since Angeline was already married to Pa's brother, and brother Ben was still a boy, she urged Ma and Pa to marry while she was still on earth. To please Nonna, they married. Nonna made a 'miraculous' recovery and lived another 21 years! From then on, every time Pa passed by Nonna's house, he did the Italian hand-under-the-chin thing. When Prohibition was repealed, Pa decided to be a tavern owner. The city issued him a license to serve liquor, but the following year, when it was time to renew the license, they discovered Pa wasn't an American citizen. Because we lived in a very liberal household, he was proud to have his name replaced with Ma's as license holder until he could produce his own citizenship papers a few years later."

Frank and Damian Schiro, sons

Baked Stuffed Eggplant

"She had a heart of gold. One day a hobo stopped at the house to ask for food. Although we had little ourselves, she removed a nice blanket from the bed and gave it to him to keep him warm at night."

1 large eggplant
4 strips bacon, diced
1/4 pound mushrooms, chopped
1 small onion, minced
1/2 green pepper, minced
1 16-ounce can tomatoes
1/2 cup diced celery
1 1/2 cup fresh bread crumbs
1 teaspoon salt
1/4 teaspoon pepper
1/4 cup melted butter
2 tablespoons grated Parmesan cheese

Cut eggplant in half; scoop out pulp, leaving 1/4-inch shell. Chop pulp. Cook bacon until crisp; remove from pan. In drippings sauté mushrooms, onions and green pepper. Add eggplant pulp, tomatoes, and celery. Simmer 5 minutes. Stir in bacon, 1/2 cup bread crumbs, salt, and pepper. Place eggplant shells in shallow pan with 1/2 cup water; fill shells. Toss remaining 1 cup bread crumbs with melted butter; press on eggplant. Top with cheese. Bake at 375 degrees for 40 minutes.

Theresa Ripp Schmelzer
December 28, 1887 - May 31, 1967

Birthplace:	Dane, Wisconsin
Parents:	Herman and Eva Hilgers Ripp arrived from Germany around 1875 and farmed in an area between Middleton and Waunakee.
Siblings:	Gerhardt, Peter, Werner, Casper, John, Joseph, Mary, Eva, Christina, Anna, and Catherine
Spouse:	Frank X. Schmelzer, born in Madison of German parents
Wedding:	1906, Holy Redeemer Catholic Church, Madison, Wisconsin
Children:	Harold "Blue," 1907; Norbert, 1910; Alfred "Whitey," 1912; Leo, 1918; Helen, 1920; Virginia, 1922; and Frank, Jr., 1928

$\mathscr{F}$ollowing the death of Teresa's mother, the family moved to Madison and into a house at the corner of Gorham and Bassett streets. Approximately three years after Teresa and Frank were married, the young couple built a home at 729 Clark Court where all but "Blue" were brought into the world. It would be the family home until Teresa and Frank passed away. The two-story wood house with a large screened front porch and two car garage still stands today. Although the yard was small, Brittingham Park and Lake Monona was within a block away and it was there where the children spent most of their time. Teresa, a fine cook and baker, set Saturday aside as her baking day. Homemade bread and coffee cake, or koffee kuchen, sprinkled with cinnamon and sugar, was the family treat after Sunday Mass. Cakes, pies, and her specialty, schaum torte with strawberries in season, were family favorites. A favorite main dish was sauerbraten. Fearing that food would be wasted if little ones helped, she did the cooking herself except on occasion when the children would peel vegetables or help in other simple ways. The growing season offered a plethora of produce for home canning, as well as making jams and jellies, and "hulling lots of strawberries."

"Mother's days were very long. The first thing she did when she got up in the morning was wash clothes in the basement. I think she had the first Maytag wringer-washer ever made. Clothes were hung on lines in the backyard. She made most of our clothes and taught me how to sew. After resting for an hour following lunch, she would begin food preparation for dinner. Meals were usually served in the kitchen, except on Sunday, or if we had company. She never knew how many people she'd be feeding because we were always bringing someone home. Considering the size of our family, there was always enough for unexpected guests. Another way of relaxing was to play cards. She loved the game, "500" and for most of her life belonged to a "500" club with her lady friends."

Helen L. Schmelzer Regan, daughter

Sauerbraten

"The house was always open, guests were welcomed, and this was one of her favorite meals."

1 1/2 cup vinegar
1/2 cup red wine
1 cup water
12 peppercorns
2 tablespoons sugar
4 bay leaves
3 onions, sliced and peeled
12 whole cloves
1 teaspoon mustard seed
2 teaspoons salt

4 pounds round or rump beef
2 tablespoons flour
1 1/2 teaspoons salt
speck of pepper
1/4 cup fat
1 onion, sliced and peeled
1/2 teaspoon mustard seed
6 whole cloves
1/2 teaspoon peppercorn
6 tablespoons flour
6 small gingersnaps

Two to four days before serving, combine first 10 ingredients in a large bowl. Set beef in this mixture, cover, and let stand for two to four days in refrigerator, turning each day. At end of this marinating period, remove meat and dry on paper toweling. Combine two tablespoons flour with 1 1/2 teaspoon salt and a speck of pepper. Coat meat on all sides with this seasoned flour. Brown on all sides in fat in Dutch oven. Strain pickling marinade Add to meat with 1 sliced onion and next 3 ingredients. Cover, simmer 3 1/2 to 4 hours or until meat is tender. Remove meat to heated platter. Strain liquid, place flour and finely crumbled gingersnaps in Dutch oven. Slowly add liquid. Simmer, stirring until thickened. Pour some of this gravy over meat, pass the rest. Makes 8-10 servings.

Note: This also can be made with leftover beef and gravy by adding equal parts of vinegar and sugar, about 2 tablespoons each. Tie 1 teaspoon of pickling spices in cheese-cloth and add to pan. Simmer slowly for 30 minutes, or so. This is good for a quick sauerbraten meal.

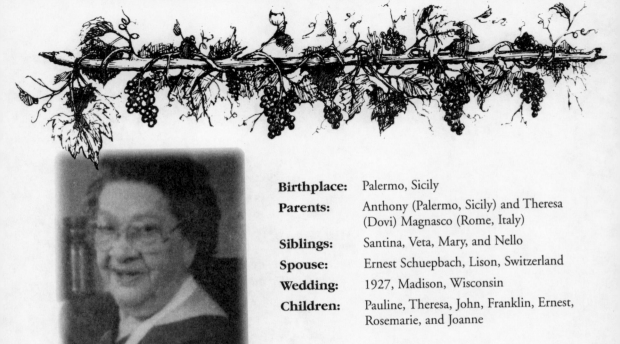

Birthplace:	Palermo, Sicily
Parents:	Anthony (Palermo, Sicily) and Theresa (Dovi) Magnasco (Rome, Italy)
Siblings:	Santina, Veta, Mary, and Nello
Spouse:	Ernest Schuepbach, Lison, Switzerland
Wedding:	1927, Madison, Wisconsin
Children:	Pauline, Theresa, John, Franklin, Ernest, Rosemarie, and Joanne

Josephine Magnasco Schuepbach
September 15, 1909 - April 3, 1992

The Schuepbachs lived beyond S. Park St. and city limits in a turn-of-the-century farmhouse. "Josie" rose early each day and often worked until late in the evening. When young men like Louis Cassini, Sam Cefalu, Sam Stassi, Ken and "Tiny" Urso, Martin Andrea, Jim and Chuck Thompson, and Charlie Harris went to the farm during the summer months to help hay and thrash straw on her days off, Josie would prepare beef stew with bologna or Italian sausage the night before to feed them the next day before they returned to their homes in the Greenbush neighborhood.

"Ma worked all the time. Back then she didn't know how to drive, so sometimes we saw her only on her day off. But when she was home, what wonderful meals she could put together with things from Pa's garden. And with such little effort. Dad would bring in vines of the cucuzza for her to make soup. Or, if the Swiss chard was ready, she'd sauté garlic in olive oil, add cleaned, cut and semi-boiled chard, add about 1 1/2 quarts of chicken broth, salt and pepper, about a pound of raw broken spaghetti, and a few tomatoes if they were handy. When it was done, she served it to us in bowls with grated Parmesan cheese. Cheese was always served with soup. Ma learned the restaurant business as a cook at DiSavlo's Spaghetti House, 802 Regent Street. When Urso's decided to leave their restaurant on W. Washington Avenue and she was given control of the kitchen with Santina and Mary, the name was changed from West Side Palm Gardens to The Three Sisters. After spending some time there, she rented the kitchen at Fedele's out on S. Park St. It was with all this love of preparing food that her restaurant (Josie's) is so successful today. It was why she eventually could buy herself a big white Cadillac."

Joanne Schuepbach Jensen, daughter

Beef Stew with Bologna or Italian Sausage

"Ma made this thin and let it boil until the guys came in from the fields..."

Fresh garlic
2 onions, cut in chunks
6 carrots, cut in chunks
1 cup celery, cut in large pieces
6 potatoes, peeled and cut in chunks
Olive oil
1 teaspoon sugar
3 teaspoons salt
1/2 teaspoon pepper
1 can of cream of celery soup
2 rings of bologna, cut in pieces,
    or Italian sausage links, See Note
1 medium can of tomatoes and juice
1 small can of peas
Grated Parmesan cheese

Sauté garlic and vegetables in oil until softened. Add seasonings and can of celery soup. Heat and add chunks of bologna and tomato chunks and water to desired thick or thin consistency. Simmer. Just before serving, add small can of peas. Heat and serve with grated Parmesan cheese.

Note: If using Italian sausage, brown lightly on both sides before adding to stew.

Birthplace:	Russia
Parents:	first names unknown
Siblings:	Nathan, Sam, and a sister
Spouse:	Ben Setlick
Wedding:	Russia
Children:	Louis, Ida, Belle, Helen, Ann, and Shirley

Ida Paley Setlick
April 4, 1885 - September 5, 1978

*F*or ten years after Ida and Ben Setlick arrived from Russia they resided in Ripon, Wisconsin. In the early 1920s, they moved to Madison and 752 W. Washington Ave. in a three-flat house owned by Mason Paley. The Appelbaum family occupied first floor and Stelicks resided on the second floor. One additional move would take Ida to the corner of 101 S. Mills St. where she would support herself by taking in roomers following her husband's death. She was proud of her home and each day swept the sidewalk that wrapped around the large corner lot. Described as being a "remarkable" woman, Ida also took great pride in her appearance, her family, and her synagogue. She was fond of all special occasions, especially bar and bat mitzvahs, family birthdays and weddings. Among some of her favorite dishes when celebrating were noodle pudding, chopped liver, spinach and beet borscht, gefilte fish, potato pancakes, cheese blintzes and apple strudel. If there was time left to relax, she sat with her needles to crochet, knit and cross-stitch.

"On March 23, 1969, the Beth Israel Center Sisterhood presented my mother with, "The Woman of Valor" award. It was the first one presented in 19 years and meant a lifetime membership for her. It truly was the greatest honor anyone could have bestowed upon her. She was humble and sincere and worked hard to devote herself to the Sisterhood in making certain she was available whenever someone needed her. The Wisconsin State Journal described her as one who symbolized 'generations of Jewish women who instilled warmth and close family ties into their homes'."

Helen Setlick Karp, daughter.

Ida's Delicious Noodle Pudding

*"She made Old Country Jewish dishes and strictly observed
Jewish religious holidays."*

1 16-ounce package wide egg noodles
6 eggs
1/2 cup sour cream, optional
Additional sour cream and/or applesauce

Prepare noodles according to directions on package. Drain noodles and add well-beaten eggs. Add sour cream to noodles, if desired. Bake in a 9 by 13-inch greased baking dish for 1 hour at 350 degrees until golden brown. Serve with sour cream or applesauce. This is also delicious when cut in squares and placed in chicken soup.

Birthplace:	Berlin, Germany
Parents:	Godfried and Wilhemina Neuman, Berlin, Germany
Siblings:	Otto, Paul, and a third brother
Spouse:	Oscar Shivers, Hillsboro, Wisconsin, African-American-Irish
Wedding:	1902
Children:	Hazel, Stanley, Nelson, Frank, Algae, and Adelin

Elsa Neuman Shivers
July 30, 1883 - April 23, 1973

The Neuman's arrived in this country in 1887, settling first in New York to farm, then moving west to Wisconsin and the rural area of Cambridge. After Elsa and Oscar were married, they purchased a large two-story building, once a store on State Street that was scheduled for demolition. Oscar had a basement dug at 11 S. Murray St. before moving the store to the Greenbush neighborhood. They were proud of their new location next to Gervasi's Store as neighbors of Felicia and Tony Pullara. The home was difficult to heat due to its large rooms and high ceilings, however, warmth was generated by the children they raised there. Elsie and Oscar would remain on S. Murray St. until the 1960s when urban renewal forced them to move elsewhere.

"With soft blue eyes and long, silky, light-brown hair, she was the most beautiful woman I have ever seen. She was an angel who could make boiled water taste good. Each morning she prepared oatmeal for her children. Homemade bread was served with an abundance of butter, and her German food drew raves. However, she was especially proud of her spaghetti sauce, having learned from Felicia Pullara next door. Another speciality was chicken, boiled, stewed, then served with homemade biscuits and nice thick gravy."

Dimetra Taliaferro Shivers, daughter-in-law

"My mother befriended UW students and Black semi-professional baseball players who visited Madison. Because there was no place for Blacks to stay back then, she made sure there was room at the house even though many had to sleep on the floor. She took pleasure in serving ham hocks, corn bread, green beans in season and, at a nickel a box, plenty of tapioca pudding. Years later, she'd be remembered during the holidays with cards of thanks for her kindness to them. She and Mrs. Pullara always seemed to have a bread-baking contest going on between them. When you opened the back door to either house, the aroma of bread baking drifted through the neighborhood."

Hazel Shivers Taliaferro, daughter

Grandmother Elsie of the Greenbush Neighborhood

*Italy probably made the most prolific contribution to the personnel of the "Bush,"
but other nations also made contributions. One person would be
Elsie Shivers, or Else, as she was named in Deutschland. Else lived at 11 S. Murray St.
and was a great favorite with both adults and children of the area.*

*In these days of ethnic and economic strife, there is no place
that offers a richer and more peaceful environment than America.
But if one is concerned with culinary delights,
American fries just do not rival German fried potatoes.*

*It is a well known fact that leftover boiled potatoes can be
sliced and fried in vegetable oil if you are very health conscious–or
pork fat, if you want something really good, the resulting dish known as
"American Fries."*

*But, if you slice raw tubers into a skillet, season just right with salt and pepper,
with a dash of onion, and fry slowly–ever so slowly–with a little
pork fat...Oh! you're in for a real treat.
Maybe you won't live to a ripe old age,
but you will be the most satisfied looking cadaver ever to elicit the common sigh,
"Don't he look natural?"*

*Else's father was a German butcher and neither he nor his daughter harbored
an excessive fear of pork fat, so they lived to be only about ninety years of age.
If you are willing to give up a few decades beyond ninety,
I offer you German fried potatoes.
Just make certain they are fried slowly to a golden brown..."*

Odell Taliaferro

Birthplace: Palermo, Sicily

Parents: Salvatore and Frances Piazza

Siblings: Joe, George, Vito, and Russell

Spouse: Frank Stassi, Palermo Sicily

Wedding: September 4, 1925, St. Joseph's Catholic Church, Madison, Wisconsin

Children: Colleen, Anthony, and Sam

Alma Piazza Stassi
August 15, 1905 - July 12, 1981

𝓕rank and Alma Stassi lived in Montalto's house at 707 Regent St., and above Troia's Market on Milton Street. It was later that Alma would open a grocery store at 502 W. Main St. and establish living quarters for the family in the apartment to the rear of the building. She enjoyed having Sunday picnics with her family at Brittingham Park.

"She used to make a stew of vegetables and eggs for supper on Fridays when we couldn't eat meat. It was delicious."

Colleen Stassi Viviani, daughter

Meatless Stew

"She had a knack for making everything taste good."

1 onion, diced
1 garlic clove, diced
3 tablespoons olive oil
3 teaspoons of oregano
2 teaspoons of garlic salt
2 teaspoons granulated garlic
Salt and pepper to taste
1 16-ounce can of tomatoes, undrained
4 sliced, peeled potatoes
3 carrots, sliced thin, optional
6-8 eggs
1 16-ounce can of peas, drained, or frozen peas
Grated Parmesan cheese

In large frying pan, sauté onion and garlic in olive oil until soft, not brown. Season with oregano, granulated garlic and garlic salt, and salt and pepper. Add tomatoes and stir to break up. Simmer, uncovered, until liquid has evaporated to half. Add potatoes and carrots. Cover and cook until vegetables are soft. Taste for seasoning and adjust accordingly. Stir in a 1/4 cup of water. Bring to simmer, then add 6 to 8 eggs, one at a time, to pan. Cover and simmer till eggs are formed and firm. Add peas (optional). Cover until peas are heated through or, if frozen, until they are cooked. Serve in bowls with grated cheese and chunks of French bread. Serves 4-6 people.

Birthplace:	Piana degli Albanesi, Sicily
Parents:	John and Maria DiModica, Italian/Albanian
Siblings:	Frank and Rose
Spouse:	Joseph G. Stassi, Piana degli Albanesi, Sicily
Wedding:	July 11, 1915, St. James Catholic Church, Madison, Wisconsin
Children:	Gaetana (Anne), 1916, and Mary, 1919

Antoinetta DiModica Stassi
March 1, 1893 - December 17, 1963

*M*aria and Joseph's children were born in the second floor apartment at the corner of Park and Regent streets. In 1923, Joseph purchased a home for the family at 527 Regent St. In 1940, they moved to 12 S. Orchard St. where they would remain until 1961.

"We all lived together in my grandparent's three flat on S. Orchard St. Nonni, Nonna, and Aunt Mary lived on first floor; my parents, brother Tony, and I lived on the second floor; and renters occupied third floor. Being together made everyday special, but holidays were the best of all. My Nonna covered the Christmas tree with presents and ornaments of angels, painted balls, glitter, and a Santa with a cotton beard. Throughout the year, I slept and ate wherever I wanted, depending on what had been prepared for supper. I recall the basement being somewhat mysterious in that something was always going on down there. There was a grape press for wine-making, and a chute to send coal through the open basement window before the house was converted to oil heat. A race track for my tricycle would be set up one day, and the next day, maybe a darkened, crepe-paper decorated ballroom for my brother's eighth grade class dance. Nonna loved having us all together. She also loved picnics and going to the stream where water bubbled and watercress grew. Other things with good memories about Nonna include her cooking styles. Carduni, mustard greens, and asparagus were collected along roadsides, and garlic and onions, in abundance, were sautéed in olive oil. And the snails...Oh! I remember them crawling out of kettles of spaghetti sauce simmering on the stove. But my favorite was, and still is, arancini. I think she probably made thousands of them in her lifetime."

Joanne Bruno Dibelius
(daughter of Anne)

Arancini

"This means 'small oranges' because the rice balls are shaped like oranges."

1 pound long grain rice
5 cups of water
1/4 cup grated Parmesan cheese
3 eggs, separated
1/2 onion, minced
garlic clove, minced
1 pound of hamburger
3 tablespoons spaghetti sauce
1 tablespoon sugar
Fresh parsley, minced, or crumbled dried parsley
1/4 cup sweet wine
Plain or seasoned bread crumbs
Oil for deep frying

Boil rice in 5 cups of water, covered, until water has evaporated, stirring occasionally. Salt to taste. When rice is cooked, add grated cheese and 3 egg yolks, reserving whites for later. Cool. Meanwhile, sauté onion and garlic; add hamburger. Add tomato sauce, sugar, minced parsley and sweet wine. Simmer until meat is cooked. Cool. Whip reserved egg whites with a fork until blended. Oil hands. Using an ice cream scoop to measure rice, place each scoop in the palm of your hand. Flatten rice and add a teaspoon of hamburger. Close and roll tightly to form a ball. Dip into egg white mixture and then in bread crumbs. Heat oil and deep fry arancini until golden brown.

Birthplace: Minsk, Russia

Parents: Samuel and Sara Sweet

Siblings: Arthur J. (A.J.), Harry, Rachel, Molly, Minnie, Mae, and Rose

Spouse: Morris Sweet, Minsk, Russia

Wedding: Madison, Wisconsin

Children: Harry, Sam, Sara, Nathan, Meyer, and Lena

Helen Sweet Sweet
March 10, 1883 - April 13, 1960

The Sweets resided at 927 Drake St., 812 Mound St., 928 Milton St., and 120 S. Murray St. Morris Sweet was a blacksmith who practiced his trade in the 700 block of W. Washington Avenue. Helen Sweet, also known as "Chaika," was a small woman with dark hair wrapped in a bun. Described as being kind and generous, "Chaika" enjoyed doing things for others. One day, while visiting her daughter, Sara Shapiro, and her husband, Sam, she learned of little Henry Cuccia's croup and pneumonia. Because he and his parents, John and Ann Cuccia, lived at the same address as Sara and Sam, "Chaika" went to work to cure him of the illness. A poultice was made by sewing two rags together before filling the handmade sack with boiled lard and onions to place on his chest. When Henry, who in adulthood became a priest, recovered from the illness, Helen felt certain it was because of the special care he received from her. It was this type of harmony in the old Greenbush neighborhood that made it as special as it was. Everyone was a friend.

"My mother used the legs of a broken chair as a T-shaped hook to lift bagels from a kettle of hot water to place on a wet board removed from the side of an apple crate. We never served them with cream cheese. Just butter and homemade jam. Picnics at Brittingham Park were special, too. It was just a block or two away—a short distance to carry food. I remember how my mother prepared food on hot summer days. We had no fans, so she'd pull the shades to keep it dark and cool as possible. She'd take off her shoes, put on an apron, and begin. When she was finished we'd have a picnic basket filled with corned beef sandwiches, watermelon, home-canned Kosher dills, dilled green tomatoes, and chocolate cake. Maybe we'd have cookies, too. Or sweet rolls from Moskowsky's. That was the Milwaukee Bakery a short distance away at 214 S. Murray St. Everything was handy in the neighborhood. There were markets in every block, meeting halls, restaurants, gas stations, synagogues and churches We had nice houses with front porches. What more could anyone want?"

Sara Sweet Shapiro, daughter

Fluffy Passover Matzo Balls

"She couldn't imagine living anywhere but Greenbush. Everything she needed was within walking distance."

2 tablespoons non-dairy margarine
2 eggs, slightly beaten
1/2 cup matzo meal
1/2 teaspoon salt
2 tablespoons soup stock or water

Mix margarine and eggs. Add matzo meal and salt. When well blended, add stock or water. Cover and refrigerate at least 20 minutes. Bring to boil 2 or 3 quarts of water. Drop hand-formed balls into boiling water and reduce flame to low. Cover and cook 30 to 40 minutes. Add to warm soup. Makes about 8 balls. Recipe may be doubled or tripled.

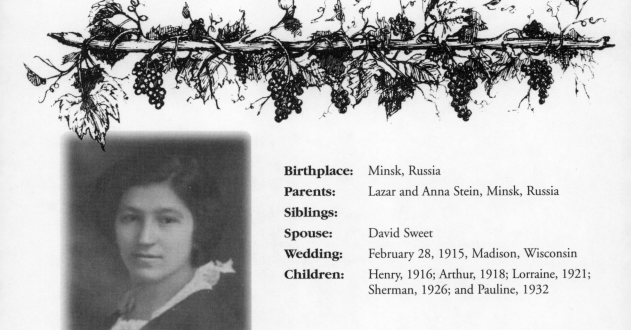

Birthplace: Minsk, Russia

Parents: Lazar and Anna Stein, Minsk, Russia

Siblings:

Spouse: David Sweet

Wedding: February 28, 1915, Madison, Wisconsin

Children: Henry, 1916; Arthur, 1918; Lorraine, 1921; Sherman, 1926; and Pauline, 1932

Ida Stein Sweet
April 2, 1893 - September 28, 1971

When David Sweet's father made his third return trip to Russia it was to gather his family to sail with him to America. The year was 1905 and David Sweet was only 14 years old. Nine years later, at age 23, David married Ida Stein, 21. They lived on W. Washington Ave. for a short time before moving to 832 Chandler St. at the corner of Chandler and S. Park streets. It is where their five children were raised. Although the home was of average size, they always made room for other family members. The large screened-in porch offered additional space for company who visited during the warm summer months.

"The house was always open. If a relative or visiting rabbi needed sleeping quarters, room was made at our house. If students needed housing, she'd take care of them. She was a hard worker. If there had been no days of Sabbath to observe, she would have worked seven days a week. It was important for my parents to live within walking distance to Beth Israel and the neighborhood markets. My mother was a very religious woman. She was also a fine seamstress and made all of my clothes. Of course, as a child, I could not appreciate that as I can today. I remember more than once wishing I could wear something store-bought. Some people purchased flour in five pound bags. Not my mother. Instead, she bought flour in 50 pound bags to use the material for making aprons. My father worked at Quality Laundry and got up each morning at 5 a.m. He'd return home at noon for dinner and again, for another large meal at suppertime."

Lorraine Sweet Borsuk, daughter

Teiglach (baked)

*"My mother's skills in the kitchen included many delicious items,
but her favorite thing to make was teiglach with honey and walnuts to serve at
weddings and bar mitzvahs."*

6 eggs
2 teaspoons sugar
3 tablespoons oil
1 tablespoon grated lemon or orange rind
4 cups of flour sifted together
    with 1 1/2 teaspoons baking powder
1 pound honey
1 cup sugar
2 teaspoons ginger
1 cup walnut meats chopped

Mix eggs, sugar, oil, rind and flour, in that order. Knead until smooth and soft and just firm enough to roll with the hands. Dough may be divided into several parts. Roll each part into a long rope 3/8 of an inch in diameter and cut it into pieces 3/8 of an inch long. While oven is heating, bring honey, sugar and ginger to a boil in a wide pan about three inches deep. Drop pieces of dough into honey mixture and put pan into a 375 degree oven. Do not open oven for twenty minutes. When pieces of dough have risen a good bit and are beginning to brown, add nuts and stir carefully. After this, stir occasionally to separate the particles. Bake for about one hour in all. The teiglach should be golden brown and feel light and hollow when stirred. Wet a board with cold water and pour the whole thick mixture onto it. Wet hands with cold water and shape quickly into a firm rectangular cake one inch high. Sprinkle with sugar and ginger. Cool, and then cut into diamond shaped pieces. These, too, will keep indefinitely, if well hidden.

From: The Jewish Home Beautiful, by Greenberg and Silverman

Birthplace: Russia

Parents: Abraham and Nashe Sweet

Siblings: Morris, Ida, Sam, William, Nathan and Louis

Spouse: Herman Sweet

Wedding: August 6, 1914

Children: Ben, Sidney and Morris

Zlote (Celia) Sweet Sweet
1891 - 1961

Zlote Sweet arrived in this country in 1913. Herman, known as "Chaim" to his friends, arrived here in 1905. He and his brother, David, were part of the original Ray-O-Vac Company staff on Regent St. near W. Washington Avenue. Later, he worked in the fruit business before establishing his own iron and scrap metal business

"Initially, my parents lived on Mills St., then later moved to a two-story home at 20 S. Orchard St. They maintained a kosher household, never eating meat outside of the home. Sabbath dinner included boiled chicken. They spoke Yiddish and English to us."

Morris Sweet, son
From "The Sweet Family, 1817 - 1991,"
by Bernard "Bud" Sweet, former resident of 811 Mound St.

Macaroni and Cheese, Passover Style

        3 large eggs
        3 1/2 cups matzo farfel (or 6 matzos, broken up)
        1/2 pound cheddar cheese
        1 cup milk or half-and-half
        1 teaspoon salt
        1/4 teaspoon white pepper
        1 pint sour cream
        1 stick (1/2 cup) butter, cut into 16 pieces

Preheat oven to 350 degrees. Grease a 2-quart casserole with butter. Beat 2 eggs well with wire whisk and pour over farfel. Cut up cheese into small pieces. Beat remaining egg with wire whisk, and stir in milk, salt, and pepper. Layer in casserole as follows: matzo farfel, half the cheese, half the sour cream (in dabs) half the butter. Distribute each layer evenly. Pour milk mixture over the top. Cover and bake for 30 minutes. Remove cover and bake 10 to 15 minutes to brown. Cut into squares. Serves 6 to 8.

From: "Something Different for Passover," by Zell J. Schulman

Birthplace: Piana degli Albanesi, Sicily

Parents: Joseph and Maria (Palermo) Masino, Piana degli Albanesi, Sicily

Siblings: Joseph and George

Spouse: Vito Traino, Sr., Piana degli Albanesi, Sicily

Wedding: April 29, 1916, Madison. It was the first marriage in St. Joseph's Catholic Church

Children: Jenny, Auggie, Russell, Michael, Vito, Jr., Angelo, Mary Jane, Joann, Joseph, Joe and George

Antonina Masino Traino
September 7, 1902 - October 8, 1967

*A*ntonina Masino and Vito Traino first met as employees of the Lorillard Tobacco Company at 651 W. Doty St. where many others from the Greenbush neighborhood worked. After their wedding, Antonina, or "Anna," and Vito resided at 119 S. Lake Street in a two-story house that exuded the wonderful flavors of the old country. It would remain their home until the neighborhood was razed in the 1960s. Small in stature, "Anna" was an energetic woman who seemed to work around the clock baking bread, canning tomatoes and other vegetables from the garden during the growing season, as well as the usual daily chores. She was one of many Sicilian women from the neighborhood who made tomato paste on boards in the sun during the hot summer months.

"She wanted the best for her children and her husband. It seemed that most of the time she was in the kitchen making pizza or other wonderful things for supper which was always served at 6 p.m. If Vito hadn't returned from work, everyone waited. They wouldn't think of having supper without him. After supper she'd rest on one of the metal chairs on the front porch where Tukya Scalissi, Rose Barbato, Daisy Caliva, and other good friends would gather to chat. During the warm months, we'd get together as a family and cook outside on the brick fireplace built along the side of the house. But wherever we ate, every meal was a celebration of family and food."

Jeni (Mike) Traino and Florence (Auggie) Traino, daughters-in-law

Rabbit Cacciatore

"If we happened to stop by after work, she always had food to send back home with us."

6 tablespoons of olive oil
4 garlic cloves
1 large onion
4 carrots, sliced
3 large tomatoes
1 8-ounce can tomato sauce
oregano
1 teaspoon sugar
1 cup water
pepper
1 rabbit, cut-up

Heat 4 tablespoons of olive oil and sauté garlic, onion and carrots. Add tomatoes and sauté. Add tomato sauce, oregano, sugar and water. Heat through. Season to taste with pepper. Brown rabbit on both sides in 2 tablespoons olive oil. Add rabbit to sauce. Cover and simmer about 35 minutes or until rabbit is tender. Uncover and continue cooking until sauce is thickened. You can also add potatoes and bake in oven until tender.

Birthplace: Trapani, Sicily

Parents: Salvatore and Maria Perlata, Trapani, Sicily

Siblings: Leonardo

Spouse: Vincent Tranchita, Pacheca, Italy

Wedding: 1900, Trapani, Sicily

Children: Anthony, Rose and Leonard

Josephine Perlata Tranchita
April 18, 1886 - May 6, 1964

Vincent Tranchita arrived first in Madison. After spending several years here, he was able to borrow money to send for his wife and Anthony and Rose, their two small children. Joining them on the voyage were their cousins, the Vultaggio's. The third floor of Corona's three-flat at the corner of Regent and S. Murray streets became the Tranchita's first apartment in the Greenbush neighborhood. Later, Vincent purchased a four-unit brick building at 815 Milton. Josephine and Vincent remained there until they were forced to leave the neighborhood in the 1960s.

"Mother was very protective of her family and shielded us from anything that seemed threatening. She was a tiny person with a high-pitched voice and a smile that accompanied every single word she spoke. She was a wonderful woman who had many friends and was very proud to be a member of the Women's Bersagliere. Although there were many small markets in the neighborhood run by nice friends and neighbors, she particularly enjoyed shopping and visiting with Mr. Navarra at his W. Washington Avenue market. Fig cookies were baked in preparation of Christmas, but chocolate was never used. Chocolate seemed to be a totally foreign ingredient in our household. Because spaghetti was served every evening for supper, she prepared it many different ways, even in soup."

Tony and Len Tranchita, son
Rose Tranchita Fiore, daughter

Fried Panfish

"Family discussions took place during supper which, by the way,
was never served until our father was seated. Once he sat down and pulled his
chair to the table, supper began."

1 pound of perch or bluegills
1 teaspoon salt
1/2 teaspoon basil
2 teaspoons parsley
1/2 cup flour
1/2 cup oil

Mix dry ingredients in a plastic bag. Add a few perch, shaking until they are coated.
Fry in hot oil.

Birthplace: Magnasco, Sicily

Parents: Giuseppe and Rosalia DiMaio

Siblings: Angelo, Dominic, Joseph, James, and a sister who served as a nun in the Vatican

Spouse: Salvatore Tripolino, Palermo, Sicily

Wedding: Sicily

Offspring: Michael, 1904, and Joseph, 1914

Catherine DiMaio Tripolino
1884 - September 26, 1937

*A*lthough four sons and two daughters were born to Catherine and Salvatore, only two sons survived. With their son, Michael, they arrived in this country in 1909. After living in New York's Little Italy for two years, they joined Catherine's brothers, Angelo and Dominic, who had arrived earlier in Madison to work as laborers rebuilding the State Capitol. The family lived together on the second floor of a three-story, cold water flat at 744 Gwinnett Court. Catherine, described as being "tiny, with lots of energy," became a widow when Salvatore died tragically in 1915. When her name is mentioned among many of the older residents of the neighborhood, she is instantly remembered with great respect as "Donna Caterina."

"I remember when she made tomato paste in the heat of summer. Wearing a long dress and straw hat, she'd select the ripest tomatoes from her staked plants. Boards used to dry the tomatoes were supported by large barrels. Many of her friends from the immediate neighborhood made paste together in the backyard. Because it was a staple in every household, the procedure was out of tradition and necessity. When my father died, it was a terrible shock for all of us. My little brother was only two. I was twelve. My mother had to work. Stripping tobacco leaves at the Lorillard Tobacco Company building behind Proudfit St. created a heavy dust inside the building, making it very unhealthy and bad for the lungs. Later, she worked as a cleaning lady at the Post Office on Monona Avenue. One day she found a dollar bill in the waste basket. Being an honest woman, she gave it to someone who worked there. She told me later that she was sure it was placed there to test her honesty. Our apartment on Gwinnett Ct. had no insulation. One winter her home-canned peaches froze on the shelf in the kitchen. Times were very tough, yet I cannot remember her ever complaining about anything. Gambinos, Ursos, Carusos and Caravellos were just a few of her closest friends. She was a wonderful woman."

Mike Tripalin, son

Fried Artichokes

"She loved sharing with others, despite what little we had."

2 or 3 lemons
Fresh artichokes
Eggs
Flour
Mazola oil
Salt and pepper to taste

Squeeze lemons into a pan of water, before adding lemons to the water. Carefully snap leaves off artichokes until yellow appears. Cut top of artichoke down to about 1 1/2 to 2 inches. Cut artichoke in half, leaving most of the stem on, and clean out fuzz by running a small sharp knife along the side. Pull purple leaves out and rinse under running water to remove any remaining fuzz. Place in lemon water to keep them from turning black while cleaning the rest. When finished, drain water and cut artichokes into sections. Pat artichokes dry with paper toweling. Beat eggs. Dredge artichokes in eggs, then flour. Fry at 360 degrees or so until golden brown on all sides. You may salt and pepper while frying. Line a pan with aluminum foil to place cooked artichokes. Cover sides with foil to keep warm until all frying is completed.

Birthplace: Gibelina, Sicily

Parents: Antonio and Catharina Lombardino

Siblings: Giocomina, Carlo, Giuseppi, Giovani Batista, Antonina, Mateo, Paolo, and Peppina

Spouse: Agostino Troia, Palermo, Sicily

Wedding: October 18, 1921, St. Joseph's Catholic Church, Madison, Wisconsin

Children: Giuseppi (Joe), 1922; Anthony (Tony), 1924; Rosina (Rose), 1925; Catharina (Kathy), 1926; Geroloma (Geri), 1928; Natale (Nate), 1930; Giacomina (Jackie), 1932; Giovani (John), 1934; Anna Agusta (Ann), 1935

Antonina Lombardino Troia
January 14, 1897 - January 16, 1980

*A*ntonina Lombardino, also known as "Lena," or "Nina," arrived in this country in 1921, the same year she married Agostino Troia. They would begin married life in a two-flat house at 919 Bowen Ct. where celebrations of life with loved ones were served with flavors of their native country and an abundance of great pride. Antonina accepted the disappointments life had in store for her, and understood with innate calmness the behaviors and lifestyles of the generations that followed.

"After our father died in 1936, we never had a Christmas tree. We were very poor and Mother could not tempt herself to celebrate the way an entire family was expected to. But holiday baking remained ever so much a part of Christmas that the kitchen was kept toasty warm from ovens that never seemed to cool. Aunt Lena Lombardino and her sister Mary Balsamo had such fun with our mother. The three laughed and chatted while carefully executing each step necessary in the making of pignolata. Now and then, they would take coffee breaks which seemed to switch conversation from food to crocheting and knitting patterns. They were masters at everything. Give them needles, yarn, and a picture and they could duplicate it without written instructions. Then they'd switch back to cooking. It was a special time for all of us. We were allowed to stay up to be a part of this holiday tradition and to watch the preparation of Sicilian holiday delicacies. During the fourth step of making pignolata, we stood close to the table to catch any of the tiny honey-coated balls if they toppled from position. Memories of Christmas remain with us today, just as memories remain vivid of Mother standing before a huge pot of spaghetti sauce or pasta e' fagioli, the favorite after-school snack for all of us and the 33 grandchildren she eventually would be blessed with."

Rose Troia McCormick and Jackie Troia White, daughters

Pasta e Fagioli

"She usually made this on a rainy day. While it cooked, we'd sing songs."

2 cups of cooked kidney beans (soak overnight and cook)
1/4 cup olive oil
2-3 garlic cloves
1 large onion, diced
2 small stalks celery and leaves, diced
2-3 ripe tomatoes, peeled and diced,
        or 1 15-ounce can of tomatoes
1 8-ounce can of tomato sauce
1 tablespoon parsley
1 teaspoon oregano
1 teaspoon dried basil
1 bay leaf
10-12 cups water or chicken stock
Salt and pepper to taste
1 cup ditalini or broken spaghetti
Romano or Parmesan cheese, freshly grated

In large stockpot, heat oil and sauté garlic and onions until soft. Add celery and cook until tender. Add tomatoes, tomato sauce, water or chicken stock, and seasonings. Simmer 20-30 minutes, uncovered. Add pasta and cook until al dente. Remove from heat. Cover and let sit about 10 minutes. Serve with grated cheese.

Birthplace: Palermo, Sicily

Parents: Frank and Theresa Caruso

Siblings: three others

Spouse: Anton Urso, Palermo, Sicily

Wedding: 1910, Palermo, Sicily

Children: Joseph, 1912, Palermo; Frank, 1913; Ernest; John, 1917; Josephine, 1920, and Anton, 1924

Rose Caruso Urso
February 14, 1887 - March 31, 1960

*A*fter Anton established a home in Greenbush for his family, Rose joined him in 1915 with their first born son, Joseph. In 1921, the Urso's moved to the upstairs apartment over Urso's Barbershop and Pool Hall at 734 West Washington Avenue. Rose was a tiny woman, weighing a mere 90 pounds. Her long "salt and pepper" hair was twirled and pinned up to be covered with a scarf or piece of material wrapped around her forehead. Described as "incredibly energetic," she worked alongside Anton, first in the barbershop and pool hall, and later, when the space was transformed to a bar and restaurant, in the kitchen preparing Sicilian food. Urso's West Side Palm Gardens became well known to university students, traveling theatre performers who gathered after show-time, and the professional workforce of physicians and attorneys in search of homemade spaghetti and meatballs, and pizza.

"Grandma's home was filled with beautiful statues and lighted candles. She also loved flowers. We remember when she took a sponge with green paint and made flowers with it on yellow painted walls. She was a great cook and made magnificent meals, especially during the holidays. The holiday table extended from the dining room to the living room to accommodate everyone in the family, plus friends Joe would invite over on a moment's notice. As the family grew, and space upstairs dwindled, our holiday dinners were set up downstairs in the restaurant. The restaurant kitchen was small, but in it were two of the largest stoves we have ever seen. It is where the best things in the world were cooked, and where the Sicilian cookies coated with sesame seeds were baked to a light golden brown."

Judy Urso Heiman, granddaughter
(daughter of Joe)

Rose Urso, granddaughter
(daughter of Frank)

Grandma Urso's Round Steak

"Holidays were the best times of all..."

Round steak
Italian bread crumbs
Olive oil
Potatoes, peeled and sliced
Salt and pepper to taste
Onion, sliced
Green pepper, sliced
Black olives
Fresh tomatoes, sliced (canned acceptable)
Grated Romano or Parmesan cheese

Pound steak and cut into serving size pieces. Dip in olive oil, then bread crumbs to coat. Fry quickly in small amount of olive oil; season with salt and pepper. Remove from pan and place in flat baking dish or pan. Add more oil to fry pan, if necessary. Add potatoes to pan and fry until light brown. Add onions and green pepper and partially cook. Place potato mixture over steak, adding black olives and sliced fresh tomatoes. Sprinkle with grated cheese. Bake uncovered at 350 degrees for 15 to 20 minutes. Serve with tossed salad, crusty homemade bread, and a bottle of red wine.

Birthplace:	Palermo, Sicily
Parents:	Joseph and Rose DiMartino, Palermo, Sicily
Siblings:	Frank, Peter, Michael, Caroline, and Josephine
Spouse:	Joseph Vitale
Wedding:	1912, St. Joseph's Church, Madison, Wisconsin
Children:	Virginia, Joseph, Frank, Anna, and Michael

Anna DiMartino Vitale
died in 1939

*I*t is unknown when Anna DiMartino and her parents arrived in this country, however the family is aware that Joseph Vitale came around 1910 or 1911 and found work with the railroad. The DiMartino and Vitale families lived next door to Frank Vitale's bakery at 114 S. Lake St. The kitchen was large as was the table where all meals were served. Anna and Joseph purchased a farm located off Fish Hatchery Road where seeds could be planted each spring for a vegetable garden. A bucket on a rope lowered into a well on the hill of the property supplied water necessary to nourish the garden throughout the growing season. Transportation when the family worked on the garden on weekends was provided by Joseph's old black Ford.

"I always called Grandma, "Ma," maybe because I spent a lot of time with her when I was young. She taught me how to cook, sew, crochet, and knit. We made tomato paste together and dried it on a board outside in the sun. She taught me how to houseclean, too. And when she was sick, I took care of everything for her. She was a wonderful person–a happy person–who had many friends. Everyone loved her. When I was married in 1932, she and Grandpa gave me a wedding shower in the bakery. Hundreds of cookies were baked with other goodies for all my friends who attended the shower. Later, special moments would include evenings and weekends when the families gathered. All the Vitale's and DiMartino's would have lunch and dinner together, ending the day by dancing and singing to piano music. The air was filled with love."

Virginia DiMartino Roan, granddaughter

Neapolitan Crostini

"I love to reminisce because it makes a day just a little bit better for me to think of the fun we used to have, and of...Grandma."

Homemade bread
Mozzarella cheese
Canned anchovies
Fresh tomato
Italian seasoning
Salt and pepper

Cut 12 fingers of bread 4 to 5-inches in length, and 2-inches wide. On each slice, place a slice of cheese, 1 or 2 anchovies, and a small thin slice of fresh tomato. Sprinkle with Italian seasoning, salt and pepper. Arrange crostini in a well-greased baking dish. Do not cover. Place in a hot oven for 10-15 minutes. Watch carefully. Serve at once while still warm. Good as a snack.

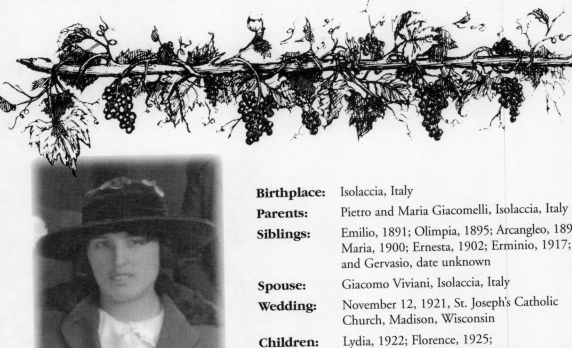

Birthplace: Isolaccia, Italy

Parents: Pietro and Maria Giacomelli, Isolaccia, Italy

Siblings: Emilio, 1891; Olimpia, 1895; Arcangleo, 1898; Maria, 1900; Ernesta, 1902; Erminio, 1917; and Gervasio, date unknown

Spouse: Giacomo Viviani, Isolaccia, Italy

Wedding: November 12, 1921, St. Joseph's Catholic Church, Madison, Wisconsin

Children: Lydia, 1922; Florence, 1925; Olga (Rita), 1928; and Peter, 1932

Olimpia Martinelli Viviani
September 18, 1895 - June 27, 1982

Giacomo Viviani arrived here in 1913 with Charlie Trameri, and Max and Pat Martinelli. Giacomo went back to Italy in 1916 to serve in the Italian army before returning to Madison on May 20, 1920. Eighteen months later, he and Olimpia, who had arrived here November 1, 1921 with Palminia and Elvira Martinelli, would share their wedding day in a double ceremony with Palminia and Max Martinelli, while Elvira and Pat eloped to Rockford, Il. The newlyweds first settled with the entire family in a home they purchased together at 18 S. Frances. Later they moved to 121 Proudfit St. In 1930, they made their final move to a newly purchased home at 1135 Emerald St. Although many of the immigrants who settled in the old Greenbush neighborhood were Sicilian born, more than a dozen families, including the Viviani and Martinelli families, emigrated from the Lombardy region in northern Italy. In 1940, Olimpia became a widow. Being forced to work to care for her children, Olimpia was hired as a housekeeper by a family that paid her 50 cents per hour. She remained with them for 25 years.

"She was a saint. I remember how tired she was when she came home at the end of the day. Yet, she never complained. We wore hand-me-down clothes, but then, everyone else was poor, too. We were blessed to have Uncle Ole (Ulysses Viviani) live with us his entire life as he took care of the things my mother was unable to. But before my father died, when we lived on Proudfit St., we had a large cool cellar where vegetables from the garden were stored with fruit my mother canned. Also stored were bottles of dandelion wine and grape wine, beer, root beer, and sausages hanging from the rafters made from pigs butchered by my father. We were close to Brittingham Park, the lake, and walking distance for weekend picnics."

Lydia Viviani, daughter

Risotto

"My mother prepared this almost every Sunday when family gathered for dinner."

2 tablespoons oil
1/2 cup chopped onion
2 cups rice (not instant)
7 or 8 cups fresh chicken broth,
  or a 49-ounce can of chicken broth
3 envelopes of saffron,
  diluted in 1/2 cup of boiling water
1/2 cup grated Parmesan cheese
2 tablespoons butter

Pour oil, onion and rice into a deep pan and brown slightly. Add 2 cups of broth, stirring constantly. Add another 2 cups of broth, etc., until all the broth is gone. Add saffron dissolved in hot water. Rice should turn a nice yellow color with a good flavor. Add cheese and butter. Mix well.

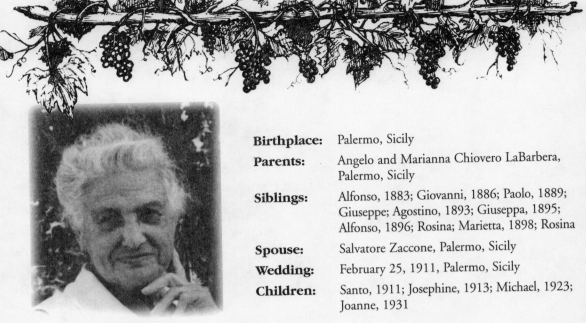

Birthplace:	Palermo, Sicily
Parents:	Angelo and Marianna Chiovero LaBarbera, Palermo, Sicily
Siblings:	Alfonso, 1883; Giovanni, 1886; Paolo, 1889; Giuseppe; Agostino, 1893; Giuseppa, 1895; Alfonso, 1896; Rosina; Marietta, 1898; Rosina
Spouse:	Salvatore Zaccone, Palermo, Sicily
Wedding:	February 25, 1911, Palermo, Sicily
Children:	Santo, 1911; Josephine, 1913; Michael, 1923; Joanne, 1931

Marianna LaBarbera Zaccone
December, 1891 - May 19, 1986

The boat carrying the Zaccone family docked in the Boston harbor in 1920. They arrived in Madison on July 25, 1921, and moved into an apartment at 740 Gwinnett Court. Other addresses in the Greenbush neighborhood would include Mound, Murray and Milton streets, before their last move to 929 Fahrenbrook Court. Mariana had attended a girl's school in Sicily for pre-teens from poor-to-average families. During her schooling she studied reading, writing and arithmetic. Also taken were courses teaching needlework and cooking. Proficient in both Italian and Sicilian, she attended classes in Madison at Neighborhood House on W. Washington Avenue to learn the language that would help mainstream her into a new life in a new country. Described as being an "adventurous spirit," Marianna longed to become either a professional seamstress or an Italian restaurant owner. However, her enthusiasm for a career never blossomed as Salvatore felt his salary at the railroad roundhouse on Regent Street was "adequate." Thus, Marianna remained at home as a wife, mother, and homemaker.

"It was too early in the century for such liberation of the Sicilian-born woman. In the early 1940s, however, the tide turned and Mother finally had the approval of my father to help nurses four to six hours a day at the local hospital. Her effusive personality and hard-working habits soon created a demand for her in various departments of the hospital, giving her a 'svago' from daily chores. It was during this time that the Circolo Da Vinci was formed. More social than literary, Italian excerpts of great literature were performed at each monthly session. Meetings were sponsored by the prominent Madison attorney, Mr. Hill, and his wife, at their home in Nakoma. Included in the small membership were Mr. Palmeri, Josephine Paratore, and others, including my sister, Josephine, my parents, and myself."

Santo Zaccone, son

Sicilian Caponatina

"As my mother wrote it, many years ago..."

1. First of all cut up the eggplant in small pieces of one inch cube. Sprinkle it with salt and let it rest for about an hour.
2. Cut up a head of celery in small pieces of about 1/2 inch size. Soak in salty water for an hour or more.
3. Wash the eggplant that has already sweated and dry it a little with a towel, otherwise it will spatter in the hot oil. Then fry it about ten minutes. Now put in the pan two or three cups of the eggplant and fry it with light oil (not olive oil, because it is too heavy.) Be sure to always turn it while frying, also to have a low heat and always stay in front of it and watch it. When the eggplant is soft and browned take them out of the pan and put in a colander so that the oil drips off and the caponatina doesn't come oily.
4. Wash celery that has already become soft, dry it with a towel and fry it in the same oil as the eggplant for ten minutes. Place in colander to allow oil to drip off.
5. Again, in the same oil, fry pitted olives (either black or green), capers (quantity at your pleasure), for a few minutes.
6. Now, take a little olive oil, sufficiently to fry the onions. Cut the onions very small, quantity at your pleasure. Depending on the quantity of eggplant etc. make a beautiful tomato sauce, Italian-style (can use fresh tomatoes), and before the sauce if fully cooked, or nearly cooked, pour into the sauce all the condiments, that is, eggplant, celery, olives, capers, etc. Cook everything for nearly about twenty or, twenty-five minutes, even half an hour, and always stir the whole mixture continuously so that it becomes thick. Put in sugar to your taste, and vinegar one-half cup or more to your taste.
7. To serve, put the caponatina in a deep bowl and on top spread toasted bread crumbs, cinnamon, and oregano. To prepare the Mollica (breadcrumbs), toast one cup of the bread crumbs and put in a dish. Now take three cloves of garlic cut fine and fried in a little olive oil. Mix together with bread crumbs that have already been toasted, add a little salt and pepper, shut off your fire, and it's done. Sprinkle over the caponatina, shaking the cinnamon and oregano over the top.

The name given this topping is "Sfingione di Melanzane" and will keep for five days.
Good Luck, Marianna Zaccone

...a Cardarella family favorite that couldn't be left out...

Mama C's Italian Olive Salad

"Mama Cardarella used to give this as a gift at informal anniversaries, wedding receptions, and birthday parties."

1 large jar or 2 cans of ripe black olives, drained
1 large jar or 2 cans of green pitted olives, drained
2 green peppers, cut in 1 1/2-inch square pieces
1 stalk of celery heart (remove leafy part),
    cut in 1 1/2-inch length pieces
2 cucumbers (pare and remove seeds and soft center),
    cut into 1 1/2-inch pieces
1 large onion, finely diced
1 garlic clove
1 teaspoon of oregano
3/4 cup olive oil
1 cup of dark vinegar

Mix all ingredients together except olive oil and vinegar. When mixed well, combine oil and vinegar and mix thoroughly with ingredients. Put in a large gallon glass jar with a cover to marinate. Refrigerate. Take out about an hour before serving to reach room temperature.

INDEX

INDEX

150

INDEX

NOTES